French in Canada

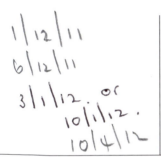

1/12/11
6/12/11
3/1/12. or
10/1/12.
10/4/12

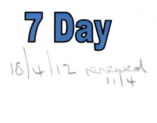

7 Day

18/4/12 renewed
11/4

University of Plymouth Library
Subject to status this item may be renewed
via your Voyager account
http://voyager.plymouth.ac.uk
Tel: (01752) 232323

Modern **F**rench **I**dentities

Edited by Peter Collier

Volume 28

PETER LANG

Oxford · Bern · Berlin · Bruxelles · Frankfurt am Main · New York · Wien

Maeve Conrick and Vera Regan

French in Canada

Language Issues

PETER LANG

Oxford · Bern · Berlin · Bruxelles · Frankfurt am Main · New York · Wien

Bibliographic information published by Die Deutsche Bibliothek
Die Deutsche Bibliothek lists this publication in the Deutsche
Nationalbibliografie; detailed bibliographic data is available on the
Internet at ‹http://dnb.ddb.de›.

British Library and Library of Congress Cataloguing-in-Publication Data:
A catalogue record for this book is available from *The British Library,*
Great Britain, and from *The Library of Congress,* USA

ISSN 1422-9005
ISBN 978-3-03-910142-9
US-ISBN 978-0-8204-6952-2

© Peter Lang AG, International Academic Publishers, Bern 2007
Hochfeldstrasse 32, Postfach 746, CH-3000 Bern 9, Switzerland
info@peterlang.com, www.peterlang.com, www.peterlang.net

Printed in Germany

Contents

Acknowledgements

This volume is the product of several years of fruitful research and co-operation between the co-authors. Maeve Conrick would like to acknowledge the financial support of the *Bibliothèque et Archives nationales du Québec*, Montreal, and the College of Arts, Celtic Studies and Social Sciences Research Fund, University College Cork. Vera Regan wishes to acknowledge the financial support of the Irish Research Council for the Humanities and Social Sciences and the *Prix du Québec* from the Government of Quebec. The authors would also like to thank the Canadian Embassy, Dublin, for their ongoing support, Dr André Lapierre, Dr Margaret Moriarty, and Dr Shana Poplack of the University of Ottawa, Dr Maurice Basque, Directeur, Études acadiennes, Université de Moncton and Dr Raymond Mougeon, University of York for their help and advice. Finally, we are grateful for the attention given by Dr Peter Collier, Editor of the *Modern French Identities* series and Dr Graham Speake at Peter Lang. Any deficiences or errors are entirely the fault of the authors.

Tables

1 Historical perspectives

New France

The adventure of French in Canada, and indeed in North America, is close to five hundred years old, having begun with the historic first voyage of Jacques Cartier in 1534.[1] On the twentieth of April of that year, Cartier left the French port of Saint-Malo and arrived in July on the east coast of Canada (Newfoundland, Labrador). Subsequently, during his second voyage in 1535, Cartier explored, for the first time, the mouth and shores of the St Lawrence River, going up river as far as present-day Quebec and Montreal.[2] Cartier took possession of Canada in the name of the King of France, thus making France the European state with the longest history in the Gulf of St Lawrence from the sixteenth century. Cartier's initial impressions of Canada were not very positive (see Ray, 2002: 2), but, nonetheless, his arrival on the shores of the St Lawrence was the beginning of an initiative that had far-reaching consequences for the continent.

Though the first arrival of French-speaking people in Canada dates back to the sixteenth century, permanent settlements were not established there until the seventeenth century, initially in Acadia (in present-day Nova Scotia), from 1604.[3] The founder of the first French settlements was Samuel de Champlain, from the Saintonge region in

1   The aim of this chapter is to provide a background to some of the important events that shaped the French presence in Canada from a linguistic point of view. For extended treatment of the history of Canada see, for example, Brown (1988 and 2002), Institute for Research on Public Policy (1999) and for the history of Quebec, Dickinson and Young (2003) and Lacoursière (1997).

2   Cartier named the river the St Lawrence, in honour of the saint on whose feast day he discovered it.

3   In 2004, the Congrès mondial acadien, which takes place every four years, celebrated the four hundredth anniversary of the arrival of the French in Nova Scotia, the cradle of Acadian culture (see www.cma2004.com).

western France. He founded the first French city of North America at Quebec on the third of July 1608, referring to it as the 'Abitation de Québecq'.[4] The city was founded on the site of the present-day church of Notre Dame des Victoires, in the Place Royale, in Vieux-Québec. The name Quebec comes from the Algonquian form *kebec*, meaning 'place where the river narrows'. Champlain called the region the Kingdom of Canada, from the Iroquoian word 'kanata', meaning 'village' or 'settlement'. As a result of his pioneering work, Champlain became known as the Father of New France (*Père de la Nouvelle-France*).[5] Trois-Rivières was founded in 1634 and Montreal (originally Hochelaga) in 1642. These settlements marked the beginning of French colonisation in America.

Champlain's idea was to build an economy based on the fur trade and the tilling of the soil by French settlers. Dickinson and Young suggest that colonisation proceeded more smoothly in the St Lawrence Valley than it did farther south, due to the fact that the St Lawrence Iroquoians had left, for reasons which historians and archaeologists have not been able to explain fully.

> Whatever the cause, their [the St Lawrence Iroquoians] disappearance meant that the French, unlike the British colonists further south, did not encounter a large, well-established, sedentary local native population when they settled the St Lawrence Valley early in the seventeenth century. (Dickinson and Young (2003: 18)

The first French immigrants to New France, Louis Hébert, his wife Marie Rollet, their children, and daughter Guillemette's husband,

---

4   The spelling of Quebec took various forms, including Quebecq (1601), Quebec (1603), Kebec (1609), and, twenty years later, Cabecke or Kabecke. (For further information on the forms and evolution of the toponym, see Quebec. Commission de Toponymie, 1996: 559.)

5   The Bibliothèque nationale du Québec holds an important collection of Champlain's maps, including his 'Abitation de Québecq' of 1613 (catalogue number RES AD 201) and his famous 1632 map of New France (catalogue number G3400 1632 C43). A full catalogue of the old maps held by the Bibliothèque nationale du Québec is contained in Lépine's (1994) *Cartes anciennes, cartes originales ou reproduites.*

Guillaume Couillard, arrived in 1617.[6] For several years, these were the only immigrants. By the 1660s, however, the numbers in the colony had increased considerably, due to a robust policy in France of encouraging emigration to New France. Immigrants included disbanded soldiers, agricultural workers and the famous *filles du roi*, who redressed to some extent the large gender imbalance. About 770 *filles du roi* arrived between 1663 and 1673, many helped by a dowry from the king (hence the appellation given to them) and almost all married within weeks or months.

The religious orders played a very important role in the establishment of New France. The religious communities which arrived included the Jesuits, the Récollets, the Ursulines and the Hospitalières. Marie de l'Incarnation, of the Ursulines, founded the first school for girls in North America, in Quebec, in 1639. Twenty years later, in 1659, Mgr François de Laval was appointed as the first French bishop in North America. The Seminary of Quebec, forerunner of the Université Laval, was founded in 1663; it was the first institution of Higher Education in French Canada. By the beginning of the eighteenth century, the French colony of New France covered a vast territory, extending south from Labrador and Newfoundland to Louisiana,[7] and west from the border with the English colonies on the east coast, across both banks of the Mississippi.[8]

---

6   The Musée de l'Amérique française in Quebec City has on display an exhibition which provides a wealth of information on the family, their history and way of life.

7   Louisiana was eventually sold for fifteen million dollars to the United States, by Napoleon, in 1803. The two hundredth anniversary of the sale was commemorated in what the French newspaper *Le Monde* described as a low-key ceremony on 20 December 2003 in New Orleans, (see, 'Discret bicentenaire de la vente de la Louisiane aux Etats-Unis', *Le Monde*, dimanche 21 – lundi 22 décembre 2003). The ceremony was attended by the President of the Assemblée nationale, Jean-Louis Debré, representing France.

8   See the map of 1756 by Jean Baptiste Nolin, 'Carte du Canada et de la Louisiane qui forment la Nouvelle France, et des colonies anglaises', Bibliothèque nationale du Québec, catalogue number G3300 1756 N6.

Much of the early history of European influence in North America is concerned with struggles between the two colonising powers, British and French. The British set up permanent colonies in North America around the same time as the French in Canada, i.e., early in the seventeenth century. It was inevitable that their competing interests would clash and that a determination would be reached in relation to who would control Canada, and indeed much of the rest of North America. Though control of territories changed hands on many occasions, France eventually ceded Acadia to the English as a consequence of the Treaty of Utrecht in 1713. A decisive point was reached in 1759, when the British army under General James Wolfe defeated the French led by General Louis-Joseph Marquis de Montcalm at the battle of the Plains of Abraham, and captured Quebec after a long and arduous siege. What was left of the French army retreated to Montreal, but the following year, Montreal surrendered. These events, referred to as *la Conquête* (The Conquest), meant that the collapse of French power was inevitable; the French became a defeated people[9] (see Moore, 1988: 174–80). As a result of the Treaty of Paris in 1763,[10] New France ceased to exist and a new British colony, the Province of Quebec,[11] was created and its inhabitants became British subjects. The Royal Proclamation of 7 October 1763 defined the new administrative structures for the province. The territory of the Province of Quebec was much reduced from the vast territory which New France had occupied:

> ... la province de Québec créée en 1763 est réduite aux deux rives du Saint-Laurent... Organisée autour de Québec, Trois-Rivières et Montréal, la province

9   All that remained of French power in North America were Saint-Pierre-et-Miquelon, Guyana, Saint Lucia and Guadeloupe. McLynn (2005) suggests that the Plains of Abraham was not only a pivotal event in Canada's past, but that it was also a turning point in world history, marking the birth of the British Empire and laying the foundations for the global dominance of the English language.

10   There is a touch of irony in the fact that the Treaty of Paris, which made Canada British, was written in French.

11   See Thos. Kitchin's map of the Province of Quebec, Bibliothèque nationale du Québec, catalogue number G3450 1764 K5.

de Québec est l'ombre famélique de l'ancienne Nouvelle-France dont le coeur était le centre même du continent.[12] (Vaugeois, 2000: 60–1)

The linguistic composition of New France

The Canada that Cartier explored during his voyages beginning in 1534 was already a very multilingual place. The native peoples spoke languages from several different language families, as well as many varieties of those languages. The language families represented in various parts of Canada at the time of the arrival of the first Europeans included: Algonquian, Iroquoian, Eskimo-Aleut, Siouan and Athabaskan.[13] The number of inhabitants was relatively small, perhaps 300,000 according to Ray (2002:12), and the population was distributed somewhat unevenly across the regions, with most concentrations along the bays and rivers, like the St Lawrence.[14] In the (present-day) Maritime Provinces, where Cartier first arrived, the main language family was Algonquian, which includes the Micmac and Cree-Montagnais languages.[15] The influence of Algonquian has left its mark, not only in Canada, but in North America generally, especially in place names such as Ottawa, Massachusetts, Illinois and Michigan.

There has been considerable debate about the linguistic competence in French of the early colonists. It has been suggested that, before arriving in Canada, many of them did not speak French, but rather one of many dialects or regional languages, because they came from a rural and socially modest background.[16] Mougeon (2000: 33–

12   'The Province of Quebec created in 1763 was reduced to the two shores of the St Lawrence… Organised around Quebec, Trois-Rivières and Montreal, the Province of Quebec was only a pale shadow of the former New France, the heart of which had been the very centre of the continent.'
13   See Rood (1992: 110–118) for a detailed description of North American languages.
14   Ray (2002) provides a detailed description of the peoples who inhabited North America at the time of the arrival of the first Europeans.
15   See Goddard (1992: 44–8) for further information on the Algonquian languages.
16   For discussion of this issue see, for example, Mougeon (2000: 33–4) and Walter (1998: 223–4).

4) contests this and argues that new research proves that in fact a large number of them did know French before they left France.

Mougeon's arguments may be summarised as follows:

- More than 90% of them came from the northern half of France.[17]
- 70% of women and 47% of men came from an urban background.
- The majority were educated.
- More than a third were of a social background, or engaged in a profession, which would have necessitated a good knowledge of French.

Mougeon points out also that the linguistic diversity (*patois*), which characterised the colonists, faded more quickly than in France and that the French spoken in New France became homogenised, precisely because colonists needed the common language of French, in order to communicate with each other.

> L'unification linguistique de la Nouvelle-France s'est traduite par l'émergence graduelle d'une variété de français homogénéisée, qui est devenue plus tard le français québécois moderne.[18] (Mougeon, 2000: 35)

From the Province of Quebec to Confederation

The Province of Quebec

When Quebec became a British colony in 1763, it might have seemed inevitable that it would eventually become English, as had happened to the Dutch colonists in New York and the Swedes in New Jersey. However, the Quebec Act of 1774 recognised some important rights

---

17 This meant that the dialects they spoke were of 'langue d'oïl' (the group to which French belonged) rather than 'langue d'oc' origin.

18 'The linguistic unification of New France resulted in the gradual emergence of a homogenised variety of French, which later became modern Quebec French.'

16

and traditions of the French-speaking population, including language and religious rights and the right to retain the civil law code. These concessions and other provisions of the Quebec Act were fiercely resented by the inhabitants of the American colonies to the south. This led to attacks by two armies of the American colonies on Quebec in 1775, though they were forced to withdraw, removing any immediate threat of another invasion. At the end of the War of Independence, in 1783, when the American colonies achieved their independence from Britain, the Treaty of Versailles was signed. This event had important consequences for the whole of North America. After 1783, many British loyalists moved north, settling to the west of Quebec, in present-day Ontario.

Upper Canada and Lower Canada

In 1791, the Constitution Act created two new entities: Lower Canada, from the old French colony of Quebec, and Upper Canada, now Ontario.[19] The Constitution Act did not address the language issue. Naturally, the issue arose when the legislative assembly of Lower Canada met on 17 December 1792, as the vast majority of deputies were *Canadiens*,[20] i.e., French-speaking, rather than English (Vaugeois, 2000: 65–7). Following a lengthy debate, it was decided that English and French would be used in the Chamber. This applied from 1792 until the Act of Union, in 1840, which prescribed English

---

19   See map of Upper and Lower Canada, 1838, Bibliothèque nationale du Québec, catalogue number G3400 1838 U66 CAR.
20   The term 'Canadiens' was used to denote the descendants of the original French colonists who had settled in New France during the seventeenth and eighteenth centuries. After 1820, the Canadiens began to use the term 'Canadiens français' to distinguish them from English-speaking Canadians. In his *Brève Histoire des Canadiens français*, Frenette (1998) discusses the historical progression of the various appellations used in reference to French-speaking Canadians: 'Pour être fidèle à la réalité historique, cette histoire des Canadiens français devrait débuter vers 1840 et se terminer vers 1960.' (Frenette, 1998: 10) ('For historical accuracy, this history of French Canadians should begin around 1840 and finish around 1960.')

as the official language of the legislature. The language issue was also a source of contention in the courts, where English and French coexisted for pragmatic reasons. However, because of the absence of any ruling on the matter in the Constitution Act, the legality of French was frequently called into question.

> Comme l'acte constitutionnel ne comportait aucune disposition précise à l'égard des langues ... la légalité du français comme langue des tribunaux de la colonie a sans cesse été remise en cause. En effet, trop souvent, lorsque la situation s'avérait incertaine, on s'empressait d'invoquer des motifs d'ordre linguistique, et ce, toujours en défaveur du français.[21] (Noël, 2000: 77)

Act of Union 1840

Further structural change took place in 1840, when the Act of Union fused Upper Canada and Lower Canada.[22] Events leading up to the Union included the ill-fated rebellion in Quebec led by Louis-Joseph Papineau and his followers, the *Patriotes*, which began in 1837. The rebellion was put down very quickly and Lord Durham, who was sent to investigate, concluded that the unrest was the result of racial struggle.

> I expected to find a contest between a government and a people: I found two nations warring in the bosom of a single state: I found a struggle, not of principles, but of races; and I perceived that it would be idle to attempt any amelioration of laws or institutions, until we could first succeed in terminating the deadly animosity that now separates the inhabitants of Lower Canada into the hostile divisions of French and English. (Durham, 1902 [1839]: 9)

21 'As the Constitution Act did not contain any precise measure concerning language... the legality of French as a language of the courts in the colony was constantly challenged. In fact, too often, when the situation was uncertain, linguistic grounds were cited readily, always to the disadvantage of French.'

22 See map of Canada East, formerly Lower Canada, Bibliothèque nationale du Québec, catalogue number G3450 1840 C35 CAR.

18

The Durham Report (1839)[23] recommended uniting the two colonies, with the intention of making French Canadians a minority and consequently, favouring their assimilation. Lord Durham believed that the achievement of this objective was only a matter of time and that it was, indeed, in the best interests of the people, because of the anglophone nature of North America.

> And is this French Canadian nationality one which, for the good merely of that people, we ought to strive to perpetuate, even if it were possible? I know of no national distinctions marking and continuing a more hopeless inferiority. The language, the laws, the character of the North American Continent are English; and every race but the English (I apply this to all who speak the English language) appears there in a condition of inferiority. It is to elevate them from that inferiority that I desire to give to the Canadians our English language. (Durham, 1902 [1839]: 215–6)

The attitudes displayed by such comments ensured that the Durham Report became and remained a focus of anger and resentment for French-speaking Canadians. His remark that French Canadians were 'a people with no history, and no literature', (Durham, 1902 [1839]: 218) remains infamous to the present day.

> Whether federalist or separatist, French Canadians could not be indifferent to the memory of Lord Durham, who had proposed the Union as a way to destroy French-Canadian nationality. His name remains a symbol of Anglicization and of Anglophone hostility to French-Canadian distinctiveness. (Institute for Research on Public Policy, 1999: 51)

Following the Durham Report, one of the measures designed to achieve the aim of assimilation was the imposition, by the Act of Union, of equal representation in the parliament for the former Upper Canada and Lower Canada, despite the fact that Upper Canada had only two thirds of the population of Lower Canada (Institute for Research on Public Policy, 1999: 47). This numerical superiority was to change subsequently with the massive immigration of anglophones

---

23 For a French version of the report, with introduction, by Denis Bertrand and Albert Desbiens, see Durham, (1990 [1839]).

from Britain and Ireland,[24] with the result that, by the time of Confederation in 1867, French Canadians accounted for only about one third of the population of the new entity (Chevrier, 1997).

The language question was addressed in Article 41 of the Act of Union, which prescribed that all documents from the legislature be drafted in English only. In practice, the linguistic reality was somewhat different, in that communication with French Canadians necessitated using French in various domains, including in the legislature. One of the consequences of the Durham Report was an even greater determination among French Canadians to preserve their heritage and culture, including their language. Article 41 was eventually revoked in 1849.

Confederation 1867– the Dominion of Canada

Ultimately, neither Upper nor Lower Canada was satisfied with the Union and a new solution was sought. This new relationship was to be the pursuit of a federal relationship, or Confederation. The Constitution Act, 1867, created the Canadian federation; it again divided Ontario and Quebec into separate provinces, combining them with Nova Scotia and New Brunswick into a new political structure. It was at a conference in Charlottetown (Prince Edward Island) in September 1864 that George Brown, George-Étienne Cartier and John A. Macdonald proposed and had accepted the idea of a federation by uniting the British colonies of North America. The details of the proposal were finalised at a conference in Quebec, attended by thirty-four

---

24 See Buckner (2003) for discussion of the proportions of English, Scots and Irish immigrants to Canada at various periods during the nineteenth and twentieth centuries. Buckner points to the predominance of Irish immigrants during the 'Great Migration', (1815–1860), and to the predominance of English immigrants between 1867 and 1914: 'The English may only have formed around a quarter of the total of British immigrants coming to Canada before Confederation but they formed a clear and overwhelming majority of the much larger number of immigrants from Britain who poured into Canada between 1867 and 1914...' (Buckner, 2003: 1).

delegates, a month later.[25] The agreement provided for a federal system, with each colony to become a province, with its own government, and each province would elect representatives (by population) to a national House of Commons. The national government was to be bi-cameral, comprising a Senate as well as a House of Commons. The central federal government would handle issues of common interest such as the economy, defence and interprovincial transport, as well as the appointment of provincial lieutenant-governors. The provinces would have responsibility for social and cultural matters, such as education, health care and the administration of justice.

The British Government, anxious to strengthen British North America, was fully supportive of the proposal. Three weeks of discussions on the seventy-two resolutions of the Charlottetown and Quebec conferences took place in London in December 1866 and, on 1 July 1867, the British North America Act was proclaimed, establishing the Canadian Confederation.[26] The three existing British colonies, the Province of Canada (comprising Ontario and Quebec), Nova Scotia and New Brunswick, became the Dominion of Canada, consisting of four provinces, Ontario, Quebec, Nova Scotia and New Brunswick. Ottawa had already been chosen by Queen Victoria in 1858 to be the capital of the then Province of Canada, and the city continued to be the capital of the new Dominion of Canada after Confederation.[27] The intention of the Fathers of Confederation, as those who had participated in the negotiations became known, was to create a strong central government and thereby to favour a strong sense of nationhood among Canadians. Paquin (n.d.) expresses his view of the situation in 1867 as follows:

25 Representatives from Prince Edward Island and Newfoundland attended the Quebec Conference, though those provinces were not to join the Confederation until later, Prince Edward Island in 1873 and Newfoundland much later, in 1949.

26 Sixteen representatives from Canada, New Brunswick and Nova Scotia participated in the meetings in London.

27 Queen Victoria is reputed to have chosen Ottawa, then a lumber city, as the permanent capital rather than Toronto, Quebec, Kingston or Montreal, so as to avoid appearing to privilege Ontario or Quebec. Ottawa, though in Ontario, has the advantage of being on the river border between Ontario and Quebec.

The people living in Canada in 1867 did not yet have a strong sense of nationhood. Anglophones derived their identity from their attachment to their home province and the British Empire. In Quebec, the 'nation' was the Quebec of the St. Lawrence Valley. This state of affairs made the institutional system of 1840 unworkable. To rectify the situation the Fathers of the Confederation created a quasi-federalism or a federation so centralized that many experts labeled it a legislative union or unitary state. John A. Macdonald, a Father of the Confederation and Canada's first prime minister, gave the Dominion government extraordinary powers for a federal system in a bid to eliminate regionalism and create a new nationality.

An analysis of newspaper coverage for 1 July 1867 reveals varied reaction on all sides and in all provinces to the celebrations on the creation of the Confederation. Joseph Howe in Nova Scotia (reported by J. B. Taylor in *The Ottawa Citizen*), suggested that it should be a day 'devoted to fasting and humiliations' (*Confederation-Confédération*, 1967: 10). In contrast, The Toronto *Globe* looks forward optimistically to a bright, united – and British – future:

> ...this day the Dominion of Canada is proclaimed; and as Canadians, no longer confined within petty Provincial limits, but members of a larger nationality, New Brunswick and Nova Scotia, Quebec and Ontario, join hands, and a shout of rejoicing goes up from the four millions of people who are now linked together for weal or for woe, to work out in common the destinies of a united British America. (*Confederation-Confédération*, 1967: 19).

La Minerve views the position of French Canadians as excellent under the new arrangements: 'Comme Canadiens-Français, la position qui nous est faite dans la Confédération est excellente. Nos droits ont été reconnus dans leur signification la plus large.' (*Confederation-Confédération*, 1967: 20).[28] This view was based on the understanding that Quebec would have greater autonomy, more control over its own affairs and would therefore be in a better position to preserve its institutions and traditions. This opinion was certainly not shared by all

28 'As French-Canadians, the status accorded to us in the Confederation is excellent. Our rights have been recognised in their broadest sense.'

French Canadians, many of whom feared being overwhelmed by even more anglophone provinces.[29]

The creation of present-day Canada which began in 1867 was an ongoing process for some time after Confederation. Manitoba was created in 1870, British Columbia was admitted in 1871 and Prince Edward Island in 1873. Saskatchewan and Alberta were created in 1905, and Newfoundland was the last province to join in 1949. There have been several territorial and boundary changes, the most recent being the creation of the territory of Nunavut, from the Northwest Territories, in 1999.

Acadia

Acadia developed separately from the main area of colonisation in New France, situated around the valley of the St Lawrence. The history of Acadia and the Acadians began early in the seventeenth century, when Samuel de Champlain arrived at the île Sainte-Croix in 1604 and set up the first French settlement in North America. In the following year, 1605, he set up a trading post at Port-Royal. This was to form the nucleus of what was to become Acadia, an area which is now centred on New Brunswick, Nova Scotia and Prince Edward Island. There is not unanimity among scholars about the origin of the name Acadia. The most generally accepted version is the following:

> Selon les connaissances actuelles, le terme Acadie est employé pour la première fois en 1524 par l'explorateur Verrazano lors d'une expédition en Amérique du Nord. Arrivé dans la région actuelle de Washington en avril, il trouve la végétation abondante et surnomme l'endroit Arcadie en souvenir d'une belle région mythique de la Grèce antique. Plus tard, au xviie siècle, le terme sera orthographié sans la lettre *r* et désignera l'actuelle Nouvelle-Écosse

---

29   See Institute for Research on Public Policy (1999: 58–62) for further discussion of the range of opinions on Confederation of both French Canadians and English Canadians.

continentale, l'île du Prince-Édouard et le Nouveau-Brunswick.[30] (Landry and Lang, 2001: 9)

A large proportion of the colonists in Acadia came from the areas of Aunis, Poitou and Saintonge, in the centre and west of France (Basque et al., 2000: 22), who emigrated largely between 1632 and 1650. Walter (1998: 214–5) points out that the current population of Acadia stems from about eighty-nine families from Poitou (and some from Touraine, Berry and Brittany), who settled there during the first half of the seventeenth century. It is therefore not surprising that some linguistic traits of the speech of Poitou have been maintained in the French spoken by their descendants in the Maritime Provinces today.

The history of Acadia was somewhat chequered, as the colony was frequently under attack by English forces. It eventually became an English colony in 1713, as a result of the Treaty of Utrecht. The Acadians, despite their attempts to maintain a neutral stance over several decades, were forced to leave by the English colonial authorities during the summer and autumn of 1755, and their removal became known as *Le Grand Dérangement* or the Deportation. Moore (2002: 172–3) describes the events as follows:

> The deportation was done with astonishing speed. Once the decision had been passed – unanimously – by Nova Scotia's governing council in July 1755, Lawrence [then acting Governor of Nova Scotia] made full use of the forces Britain had amassed in Nova Scotia. A fleet of merchant ships was quickly hired and provisioned. Lawrence ordered his regiments to round up the Acadians and march them on to his ships with what baggage they could carry, and to burn the villages as soon as they were emptied. In a matter of months Acadia ceased to exist. Village by village, at Grand Pré, Minas, Beaubassin, all around the Fundy shore, at least seven thousand Acadians were seized and sent into exile before the end of 1755. Another few thousand would be exiled in the next few years. Perhaps two thousand fugitives would hold out in the woods.

---

30 'According to current scholarship, the term Acadie was first used in 1524 by the explorer Verrazano during an expedition to North America. On arrival in present-day Washington in April, he found the vegetation abundant and named the area Arcadia after the beautiful mythical region of Ancient Greece. Later, in the seventeenth century, the term was spelt without the letter r to refer to present-day continental Nova Scotia, Prince Edward Island and New Brunswick.'

The acclaimed Acadian writer, Antonine Maillet, relates the saga of these traumatic events in *Pélagie-la-Charrette*, which won the *Prix Goncourt* in 1979. They were also immortalised in Longfellow's *Evangeline*.

Some of the deported Acadians eventually found refuge in Louisiana, where they became known as 'Cajuns',[31] a form of the French word 'Acadiens', (see Conrick, 2002b: 238–9). Others were left in various places along the Atlantic coast from New England to Georgia. After the end of the Seven Years' War in 1763, small groups of Acadians, with great determination, made the journey back. However, when they arrived, they had to make new arrangements, as the fertile land that was previously theirs had been taken over by new colonists. The result was that many had to move westwards to New Brunswick.

The Deportation, despite the passage of more than two centuries, plays an important symbolic role in Acadian consciousness. On 2 December 2003, the *Société nationale de l'Acadie* succeeded in having a royal Proclamation adopted by the federal government, officially recognising the wrongs caused to Acadians during the Deportation. The then Governor General, Adrienne Clarkson, on behalf of the Queen, signed the Proclamation, which came into effect on 5 September 2004. The Proclamation also provides for an annual commemorative day on 28 July, beginning in 2005.

In 1867, Nova Scotia and New Brunswick were two of the first four provinces, along with Ontario and Quebec, to form the core of the new federation, the Dominion of Canada. In twenty-first century Canada, New Brunswick is the province which has the highest proportion of francophones, apart from Quebec.

---

31   This was in order to distinguish them from the first French colonists already settled in Louisiana, after Cavelier de la Salle had claimed it for the King of France, Louis XIV, in 1682.

Canada after Confederation

Many French Canadians were happy with Confederation, since the result was that Quebec City again became a capital, with a parliament, and the French language had political and legal status. Article 133[32] of the British North America Act established the use of either English or French in federal parliamentary debates and in proceedings before the federal courts, as well as in Quebec; the section also provided that laws would have to be enacted and published in both languages. Article 93 contained a provision, which, although not directly linguistic, had linguistic side-effects. It stated that education was the domain of the provinces, but that the latter had to respect the rights and privileges of denominational schools.

However, the position and future of French within the Canadian federation did not turn out to be secure. Assimilationist policies were pursued, for example, in the context of the school system, with much controversy being engendered by the fact that some provinces in which francophones were in the minority restricted the rights of francophones to have their children educated in French Catholic schools. Manitoba, despite having a substantial francophone population, abolished French in schools in 1890, and also put an end to the right to speak French in the legislature, despite the fact that francophone language rights had been guaranteed when Manitoba joined the Confederation in 1870. Another instance of restriction of education rights was provided by the Northwest Territories, which, in 1892,

---

32   'Either the English or the French Language may be used by any Person in the debates of the Houses of the Parliament of Canada and of the Houses of the Legislature of Quebec; and both these Languages shall be used in the respective Records and Journals of those houses; and either of those Languages may be used by any person or in any Pleading or Process in or issuing from any Court of Canada established under this Act, and in or from all or any of the courts of Quebec. The Acts of the Parliament of Canada and of the Legislature of Quebec shall be printed and published in both those Languages.' (Canada, 1867: section 133)

made English the only language of education.[33] Ultimately, it can only be concluded that Confederation did not protect the rights of francophone minorities.

A political event that underlined the lack of political clout of French Canadians across the new federation was the hanging of Louis Riel, who had led a rebellion of the *Métis* in Manitoba in 1885. The rebellion was crushed, Riel surrendered, and he was put to death by the federal government despite the protestations of Quebec. This event came to symbolise the oppression of francophones outside Quebec.

Again in the context of education, in 1913, the province of Ontario adopted Regulation 17, which restricted the rights of Franco-Ontarians to have their children educated in French. In that year, the politician Howard Ferguson, who would later become Premier of Ontario, expressed the reasoning behind this measure as follows:

> The bilingual system encourages the isolation of races. It impresses the mind of youth with the idea of race distinction and militates against the fusion of various elements that make up the population.... The experience of the United States where their national school system recognizes but one language simply proves the wisdom of the system.' (Quoted in Cook, 2002: 417)

The agenda, as expressed in the above quotation, was obviously one of assimilation, reminiscent of the Durham Report, rather than of linguistic tolerance. Not surprisingly, French Canadians in Ontario and in Quebec were outraged by this attitude and rejected it vehemently. In addition, the rights of the Anglo-protestant minority were respected in Quebec, and so there was a clear difference of treatment of minorities in Ontario and Quebec. An interesting aspect of the situation was that anglophone Catholic schools in Ontario did not receive the same treatment as francophone schools; a fact which clearly spelled out that the issue was not so much religion as language:

> ... le financement des écoles catholiques de langue anglaise est maintenu. Les Canadiens français comprennent enfin que ce n'est pas en tant que «catholiques» qu'ils ont subi, depuis 1871, toute une série de restrictions de leurs

---

33   See Harvey (2000) for further discussion of francophone minorities and the school system.

droits scolaires, mais bien en tant que «francophones».[34] (Pelletier-Baillargeon, 2000: 188)

Developments in Quebec

The period from the middle of the nineteenth century to the middle of the twentieth century was a time of important social and cultural growth in Quebec. Many educational institutions were founded, schools, universities[35] such as Laval, the first francophone catholic university in 1852, the *Université de Montréal* in 1878, *grandes écoles* such as the *École polytechnique de Montréal* in 1873 and *Hautes Études commerciales* in Montreal in 1907. There were other very significant developments in the print media such as the establishment of important newspapers like *La Presse* (1884) and *Le Devoir* (1910) and publishing houses including *L'Hexagone* (1953) and *Fides*. The population increased significantly from 890,000 to 5,259,000 and the majority, over 81 per cent, was francophone (Plourde, 2000: 137). However, three quarters of the children of immigrants went to anglophone schools, thus integrating them into the anglophone rather than the francophone population. While the idea of resistance to assimilation had previously been a characteristic of French Canadians, the emphasis moved towards the issue of survival (*la survivance*) in a minority context. As Quebec was the only province where francophones were in the majority, it occupied a central position in the struggle to uphold the interests of French Canadians. Successive Quebec governments demanded that the rights of French Canadians be respected.

The position of English throughout Canada was strong after Confederation. Even within Quebec, English had equal status and, for economic reasons, it predominated. Industrialisation and the increased

---

34   'The financing of anglophone Catholic schools was maintained. French Canadians finally understood that it was not because they were "Catholic" that they had suffered, since 1871, a series of restrictions of their education rights, but rather because they were "francophone"'.

35   McGill had been founded during the first half of the nineteenth century, in 1829.

movement of the population to the cities, especially Montreal, underlined the economically disadvantaged situation of francophones. Business was conducted through English, and French Canadians were increasingly obliged to become bilingual, thus making assimilation an even more probable outcome. It became clear that Canada was likely to become ever more anglophone. Early in the twentieth century, some progress was made towards bilingualism with, for example, postage stamps becoming bilingual in 1927 and bank notes in 1936, though these were seen by many as largely symbolic.[36] Bilingualism, as a policy, was not introduced until the 1960s, with the passing of the first Official Languages Act in 1969. The framing of legislation on language, which was to become a key feature of policy and planning in Quebec in the 1960s and 1970s, began with the first language law passed in Quebec in 1910. Called the Lavergne Law, it required that tickets for public transport be printed in French and English.

By 1960, the stage was set for an increase in nationalist sentiment, based on a policy of the autonomy of Quebec, with the advancement of the French language increasingly becoming a focus of interest and concern. French-speaking Canadians had become increasingly dissatisfied with their situation and were more prepared to pursue a nationalist agenda in order to protect their identity and promote their interests. The pursuit of these issues would lead ultimately to the 'Quiet Revolution' during the term of the Liberal government of Jean Lesage, which took office in 1960.

The Quiet Revolution and its aftermath

The social and political upheavals of the 1960s were a turning point in the history of modern Quebec. These developments are very well documented by historians, political commentators and others.[37] During the 1960s, many of the certainties of previous generations fell away.

---

36 Plourde (2000: 137) describes these two developments as 'quelques victoires symboliques', ('a few symbolic victories').
37 It is not the intention here to treat this phenomenon in detail. For fuller discussion see for example Brown (1988 and 2002), Frenette (1998), McRoberts (1999) and Dickinson and Young (2003)

The grip of the Catholic Church weakened. Nationalist sentiment in the province grew and led to an even greater sense among Quebecers of their distinctiveness as a society. This change was symbolised linguistically by the fact that Quebecers abandoned the term previously applied to them, *Canadiens français*,[38] and replaced it with the term *Québécois*, thus firmly rooting their sense of identity within their province. Consequently, what had been previously a French Canadian identity became fragmented and francophones in provinces outside Quebec (*les francophones hors Québec*), were prompted to affirm their own provincially-based identity and began to refer to themselves as *Franco-Ontariens* in Ontario, *Fransaskois* in Saskatchewan, *Franco-Manitobains* in Manitoba, *Franco-Albertains* in Alberta and *Franco-Colombiens* in British Columbia.

Various social, cultural and sporting events drew international attention to Quebec in the 1960s and 1970s. These included Expo 67 in Montreal, during which General de Gaulle uttered the immortal phrase: 'Vive le Québec libre!'. There had been a renewal of links between France and the Quebec government during the 1960s, for example, the opening of the *Délégation générale* office in Paris in 1961. Quebec had begun to play a more prominent role on the international stage.

The founding (in 1968) of the *Parti Québécois* (PQ), referred to as the *péquistes*, a party with a separatist agenda, brought a new focus to the aspirations of the *Québécois*. The party came to power in the general election of November 1976 and René Lévesque became Premier. It was the first time that a party with a separatist agenda formed a majority government in Quebec. Separatism[39] gained momentum and two of the defining moments of the last two decades of the twentieth century in Quebec were provided by the referenda on

---

38   Frenette (1998: 9–10) points out that the terms 'French Canadians' and 'French Canada' can still be heard, mostly used by Anglophones, but that they are anachronisms, since 'French Canada' disappeared as an ethnic identity in the twentieth century.

39   Not all separatists used peaceful means to promote their cause: a revolutionary group, the Front de libération du Québec (FLQ) engaged in a series of criminal actions beginning with the kidnapping of a British diplomat in October 1970 (events subsequently referred to as the October crisis).

sovereignty which were held in 1980 (on Sovereignty-Association) and 1995 (on Sovereignty-Partnership). The second referendum was defeated by a very narrow margin ('no': 50.6%; 'yes': 49.4%), after a hard-fought and divisive campaign between separatists and federalists, which received wide coverage in the international media.

Equally contentious during the 1980s and 1990s were the attempts to solve the continuing constitutional crisis by negotiating a solution that would include, and be acceptable to, Quebec. Quebec stood alone among the ten provinces in not consenting to the Constitution Act of 1982. However, attempts to reach agreement did not succeed. The Lake Meech Accord (1987),[40] which included a clause recognising Quebec as a 'distinct society', failed, as did the Charlottetown Accord (1992),[41] and the constitutional debate remains unresolved.

The sweeping societal changes which began in the 1960s in Quebec inevitably had a strong impact on language and language policy. The French language was a central component of the national character of the *Québécois*, defining and underlining, as it did, their distinctiveness. Among the early developments in a more focused policy on language issues in Quebec was the establishment of the *Office de la langue française* in 1961. This institution played, and continues to play, a leading role in the promotion and development of French in the province. The 1970s saw a programme of language legislation enacted in Quebec. Language issues featured strongly at federal level also, with the setting up in 1963 of the Royal Commission on Bilingualism and Biculturalism, which gave rise to the enactment of the first Official Languages Act in 1969, an attempt to recognise the linguistic duality of Canada, based on the concept of the two founding nations. The next chapter focuses on these and related issues of language policy and planning.

40   See Institute for Research on Public Policy (1999: 315–24).
41   See Institute for Research on Public Policy (1999: 337–44).

Key Dates

1534	Arrival of Jacques Cartier in New France
1604	Foundation of a settlement on the île Sainte-Croix (in Acadia) by Samuel de Champlain
1608	Foundation of Quebec by Samuel de Champlain
·1713	Treaty of Utrecht cedes Acadia to the English
1755	'Le Grand Dérangement', beginning of the deportation of the Acadians
1759	Battle of the Plains of Abraham, Quebec
1763	Treaty of Paris: New France becomes a British colony, the Province of Quebec
1774	Quebec Act recognises religious, civil law and language rights of French Canadians
1783	Treaty of Versailles ends American War of Independence
1791	Constitution Act divides Canada into Upper Canada and Lower Canada
1837–8	Quebec Rebellion
1839	The Durham Report
1840	Act of Union fuses Upper Canada and Lower Canada
1867	British North America Act establishes the Dominion of Canada (Confederation)

1960	Beginning of 'The Quiet Revolution' in Quebec
1970	October Crisis in Quebec
1980	Quebec referendum on Sovereignty-Association
1982	The Constitution Act (incorporating the Canadian Charter of Rights and Freedoms)
1987	Lake Meech Accord
1992	Charlottetown Accord
1995	Quebec referendum on Sovereignty-Partnership

2 Language policy and language planning at the Federal level

Introduction

Following the Quiet Revolution in Quebec in the 1960s, language issues came increasingly to the fore, with Quebecers becoming more demanding in respect of their rights in this as in other areas. It was clear that French-speakers in general in Canada were economic under-dogs and that, even in Quebec where they were a very substantial majority, their economic status was much lower than that of English speakers. In Montreal the top positions were occupied by Anglo-phones, who constituted only about twenty per cent of the population. The most poorly paid workers were French-speakers, who were hampered by the need to use a second language at work, and who lagged behind most major ethnic groups in financial terms. Many *Québécois*, as they had redefined themselves, worried about losing their language and identity and believed that the only way forward for them was to pursue a Quebec nationalist agenda.

It was clear that the situation could not continue as it was and that the federal government would have to take steps to respond to *Québécois* demands, which were becoming more vociferous, if the very integrity of the Confederation was not to be undermined and threatened. One response to the increasing unrest in Quebec and the consequent tensions between the province and the rest of Canada was to set up a Royal Commission.[1] The Royal Commission on

---

1   The function of Royal Commissions is to investigate issues which have national implications. Fox (1999: 2045) introduces his discussion of Royal Commissions as follows: 'Royal Commissions, once described by a member of Parliament as costly travelling minstrel shows, are a form of official enquiry into matters of public concern. They descend from the British monarch's prerogative power to order investigations...'

Bilingualism and Biculturalism ('The B&B Commission') was duly established to investigate and write a report. It represented a defining moment in terms of the principle of the cultural and linguistic duality of Canada and ushered in a whole new era of language policy.

The Royal Commission on Bilingualism and Biculturalism

The B&B Commission, set up in 1963 by the Liberal Prime Minister Lester B. Pearson, was co-chaired by André Laurendeau, editor in chief of *Le Devoir* since 1957, and A. Davidson Dunton, President of Carleton University, who had previously been a journalist and the first full-time Chairman of the Canadian Broadcasting Corporation (CBC). The Commission is sometimes referred to by the names of its co-chairs as the Laurendeau-Dunton Commission. The full list of Commissioners was:[2]

- André Laurendeau, Montreal, Quebec
- A. Davidson Dunton, Ottawa, Ontario
- Clément Cormier, Moncton, New Brunswick, (cleric and academic)
- Royce Frith, Toronto, Ontario, (lawyer and politician)
- Jean-Louis Gagnon, Montreal, Quebec, (journalist and writer)[3]
- Gertrude M. Laing, Calgary, Alberta, (educator)
- Jean Marchand, Quebec, (Secretary General of the *Confédération des travailleurs catholiques du Canada*)[4]
- J. B. Rudnyckyj, Winnipeg, Manitoba, (academic)
- Frank R. Scott, Montreal, Quebec, (poet and educator)
- Paul Wyczynski, Ottawa, Ontario, (academic)

---

2   See Royal Commission on Bilingualism and Biculturalism, (1967: Appendix 1) for details of the appointment of the Commissioners.
3   Gagnon took over as co-chair after the death of Laurendeau in June 1968.
4   The resignation of Marchand was accepted on 21 September 1965 and one of the co-secretaries of the Commission, Paul Lacoste, was appointed in his place.

The choice of members was intended to represent the cultural and linguistic composition of Canada, though in the West the Commission was seen as responding to matters of concern to eastern Canada. Five of the Commissioners were predominantly French-speaking and five were predominantly English-speaking. In the choice of members, an attempt was made to represent the other language groups of Canada by the appointment of a Commissioner of Ukrainian descent (Rudnyckyj) and another of Polish descent (Wyczynski). Michael Oliver, Research Director to the Commission, in his reflections on the workings of the B&B Commission, takes the view that Montreal was overrepresented, as five of the ten Commissioners (Laurendeau, Dunton, Frith, Scott and Gagnon) had Montreal connections:[5]

> ... the Commission overrepresented the city of Montreal much more seriously than Central Canada itself; and it has always surprised me that this anomaly received so little attention. [...] Obviously, there was no lack of understanding of the nuances of living in two solitudes, and I personally think the Commission was none the worse for it. (Oliver, 2001: 2)

The brief of the B&B Commission was to:

> inquire into and report upon the existing state of bilingualism and biculturalism in Canada and to recommend what steps should be taken to develop the Canadian Confederation on the basis of an equal partnership between the two founding races, taking into account the contribution made by the other ethnic groups to the cultural enrichment of Canada and the measures that should be taken to safeguard that contribution ... (Royal Commission on Bilingualism and Biculturalism, 1967: Appendix 1)[6]

The B&B Commission worked on the premise that partnership – especially 'equal partnership' – should characterise relations between French and English Canadians. This was evident from the beginning in the terms of reference and had the advantage of avoiding the use of terms like 'minority' and 'majority'.

---

5   He also refers to his own Montreal connections and to those of one of the Commission's co-secretaries, Paul Lacoste, and to the fact that the other co-secretary, Neil Morrison, had spent many years at McGill.

6   Oliver (2001: 6) notes that the Commission itself used the term 'peoples' rather than 'races' and that in French the term 'peuples' was used.

The B&B Commission began its work in November 1963 and held hearings across the country, in English and French, consulting widely with Canadians over the following six years.[7] A Preliminary Report was released in 1965, which observed that 'Canada, without being fully conscious of the fact, is passing through the greatest crisis in its history', and that:

> it would appear from what is happening that the state of affairs established in 1867, and never since seriously challenged, is now for the first time being rejected by the French Canadians of Quebec. (Royal Commission on Bilingualism and Biculturalism, 1965: 13)

The federal government and the provinces were criticised for failing to protect the rights of French Canadians, since, for example, English was the working language used by federal institutions and provincial governments had not fulfilled their obligations to francophone minorities. Book 1 of the B&B Commission's report was presented in 1967 and dealt with *Official Languages*. Book II on *Education* appeared in 1968 and discussed in particular the following questions: instruction of the francophone or anglophone minority in each province and the teaching of the second language, English or French.[8]

The final report in six books contained a hundred recommendations intended to redress some of the many shortcomings of the *status quo*, which had been identified by the B&B Commission. G. Laing outlines the main findings as follows:

> The enquiry [...] revealed that Francophones did not occupy in the economy, nor in the decision-making ranks of government, the place their numbers warranted; that educational opportunities for the francophone minorities were not commensurate with those provided for the anglophone minority within Québec; and that French-speaking Canadians could neither find employment

---

7   The archives of CBC contain television and radio clips relating to the Commission's work and reactions to it. (See http://archives.cbc.ca/IDD–1–73–655/politics_economy/bilingualism/)

8   The other four books of the report were published as follows: Book III, *The Work World* (1969), Book IV, *The Cultural Contribution of the Other Ethnic Groups* (1969), Book V, *The Federal Capital* (1970) and Book VI, *Voluntary Associations* (1970).

nor be served adequately in their language in federal-government agencies. (Laing, 1999: 235)

In its recommendations, the B&B Commission opted for policies promoting bilingualism, such as the adoption of a law on Official Languages and the extension of official bilingualism to the federal government. This view of the situation was a defining factor in the subsequent development of policy on language in Canada. In 1969, the federal government of Pierre Elliott Trudeau (who had become Prime Minister in April 1968) introduced the first Official Languages Act, making both English and French official languages of Canada, thereby imposing obligations on federal institutions to provide services in both languages. The Act also created the post of Commissioner of Official Languages.[9] The Commissioner currently acts as an agent of change and as a kind of ombudsperson, who is charged with promoting the equality of the official languages throughout Canadian society, ensuring the equality of both languages in Parliament, in the federal administration and in institutions subject to the Act, and with investigating any complaints about the implementation of the Act.[10] The enactment of the Official Languages Act is generally considered to be the most important direct result of the B&B Commission's work.[11] The Act implemented recommendation twelve of Book 1 of the Report:

9   The second Official Languages Act in 1988 reinforced the role of the Commissioner. The Commissioner of Official Languages from 1999 to 2006 is Dr Dyane Adam.

10   The Canadian model of legislation for Official Languages has influenced language policy internationally. For example, Ireland passed an Official Languages Act (Ireland, 2003) which makes similar provisions to those in the Canadian legislation (Official Languages Acts 1969 and 1988) including the setting up of the Office of the Official Languages Commissioner (An Coimisinéir Teanga), with a mandate akin to that of the Canadian Commissioner. Section 20 of the Act provides that: 'The Commissioner will be independent in the performance of his or her duty and will be appointed by the President.'

11   The Commissioner of Official Languages describes it as 'the B&B Commission's most-noteworthy product' and her role as that of 'guardian' of the Act (Canada. Commissioner of Official Languages, 2003a). She also identifies 'three other immediate results, or outcomes that are directly attributable to the

> We recommend: a) that Parliament adopt a law on the official languages; b) that the Governor General in Counsel designate a Commissioner General of official languages responsible for overseeing respect for the status of French and English in Canada. (Royal Commission on Bilingualism and Biculturalism, 1967: 148)

In another recommendation on official languages, the Commission urged the governments of New Brunswick and Ontario to declare themselves officially bilingual. New Brunswick complied with the recommendation, passing the Official Languages of New Brunswick Act in 1969; Ontario did not.

One of the B&B Commission's recommendations on Education (Recommendation thirteen, Book II) envisaged a dual educational structure in the provinces. In contrast to the high level of acceptance of the recommendations on Official Languages, the area of education was controversial and contested. Though the Commission's recommendation was adopted in New Brunswick in 1973, other provinces have been slow to make equitable provision, though some progress has been made. In many cases, education rights were provided only after legal action required compliance with the rights guaranteed under the Canadian Charter of Rights and Freedoms of 1982 (discussed below). The Commissioner of Official Languages indicates that 'the implementation of language rights in education is not yet fully completed and progress has been variable across the country'. (Canada. Commissioner of Official Languages, 2003a).

In Book V of its Report (*The Federal Capital*), the B&B Commission emphasised what it saw as the particularly important symbolic role of the federal capital area in realising the bilingual ideal, in the following terms:

> We recommend, for the present federal capital and areas to be designated as part thereof, that the French and English languages have full equality of status, and that the full range of services and facilities provided to the public be available in both languages throughout the area. (Royal Commission on Bilingualism and Biculturalism, 1970, Book V: 41)

B&B Commission's work', i.e., the raising of popular awareness, the wealth of research produced and the multiculturalism policy.

The Commission's ideals were indeed lofty, and, forty years later, when principle is compared with practice, the reality may be found to fall far short of that ideal. Much attention is paid at present, in the early twenty-first century, to official languages in the National Capital Region (NCR), though opinion is divided about the level of success in achieving the ideals set out by the Commission. One report on the application of the Official Languages Act to the NCR, that of the Parliament's Standing Joint Committee on Official Languages, while presenting a positive picture of the federal government's endeavours, makes a number of recommendations for improvement.[12] The *Bloc Québécois* adds a dissenting opinion in which it trenchantly points out:

> the failure of the federal language policy [...] [which] is all the more resounding since it takes place in Canada's capital, which should be a better reflection of linguistic duality than any other location in Canada. (Canada. Standing Joint Committee on Official Languages, 1997)

The Commissioner of Official Languages in her Annual Report for 2002–2003, published in October 2003, refers to the NCR under the heading: 'Bilingualism in the National Capital: What is the province waiting for?' The City of Ottawa was restructured in 1999, and she takes issue with the Government of Ontario for its 'inaction' in not amending the 'provincial Act creating the new city, so that it could become officially bilingual' (Canada. Commissioner of Official Languages, 2003b: 115). This view gives rise to Recommendation 7 of the Commissioner's Report: 'The Commissioner recommends that the Minister Responsible for Official Languages: Examine and take all measures available to him so that the capital of Canada will be

---

12 The Standing Joint Committee lists some of those consulted during the preparation of the report as: the Minister of Canadian Heritage, the Chairman of the National Capital Commission, a senior official of Public Works and Government Services Canada, the Commissioner of Official Languages, representatives of the Fédération des communautés francophones et acadienne du Canada, the Ottawa–Carleton regional chapter of the Association canadienne-française de l'Ontario, the City of Ottawa's Advisory Committee on French-Language Services, the Mouvement Impératif français and the Outaouais Alliance (see Canada. Standing Joint Committee on Official Languages, 1997).

declared officially bilingual' Commissioner of Official Languages, 2003b: 116).

With regard to the fate of the 'bicultural' element of the B&B Commission's brief, the government quickly replaced the term with 'multicultural', which fitted more closely with Trudeau's espousal of multicultural policies. Legislation on multiculturalism was introduced in 1971. Trudeau's vision of Canada was very much a bilingual and multicultural one: he vehemently opposed Quebec nationalism during his entire political career and was deeply committed to preserving the integrity of Canada. The pursuit of a policy of national bilingualism was one way of undermining the attraction of Quebec nationalism. Trudeau's views in this area are summarised by one commentator in the following terms:

> He believed that in a country like Canada, with two large linguistic groups, it was common wisdom that language, ethnicity and culture should be de-politicized and understood as individual rights. [...] He was mostly concerned with Quebec nationalism which he spent his whole career fighting. He wanted Quebeckers to identify with Canada, not with the province of Quebec. (Cardinal, 2003: 9)

The Report of the B&B Commission was an important milestone in language policy and planning in Canada, with far-reaching political as well as linguistic consequences. The Commission's analysis and recommendations were the first serious attempt in Canada to tackle issues which had reached crisis point. It represented a crucial development in language planning, in that it provided an impetus for the development of language policy at both federal and provincial levels.

The Canadian Charter of Rights and Freedoms

The first Official Languages Act of 1969 was a major piece of legislation governing language rights at the federal level. Other very significant measures, with implications for language rights, were to follow, in particular the Constitution Act 1982, which incorporated the Canadian Charter of Rights and Freedoms ('The Canadian Charter') (Canada. Department of Justice, 1982). The Constitution Act was the result of the patriation of the Canadian Federation's Constitution to Canada from the British Parliament in Westminster. The Canadian Charter, by giving constitutional status to language issues and guaranteeing language education rights to provincial minorities, placed language rights at a higher level, with the result that major cases were taken to and determined by the highest court in the land, the Supreme Court of Canada. All provincial laws were now subject to the Constitution and could be overturned if found to be inconsistent with it. This meant a considerable loss of power on the part of the provinces. Despite the fact that the province of Quebec did not give its consent to the patriation and promulgation of the 1982 Constitution, it became subject to its provisions.

The Canadian Charter contains sections that deal specifically with language rights. Sections 16 to 22 deal with the Official Languages of Canada. These sections strengthen the provisions of the 1969 Official Languages Act, by entrenching them firmly in the Constitution. Some of the provisions are as follows:

16 (1) English and French are the official languages of Canada and have equality of status and equal rights and privileges as to their use in all institutions of the Parliament and Government of Canada. [...]
17 (1) Everyone has the right to use English or French in any debates and other proceedings of Parliament. [...]
18 (1) The statutes, records and journals of Parliament shall be printed and published in English and French and both language versions are equally authoritative. [...]

19 (1) Either English or French may be used by any person in, or in any pleading in or process issuing from, any court established by Parliament. [...][13]

20 (1) Any member of the public in Canada has the right to communicate with, and to receive available services from, any head or central office of an institution of the Parliament of Canada in English or French, and has the same right with respect to any other office of any such institution where there is a significant demand for communications with and services from that office in such language; or due to the nature of the office, it is reasonable that communications with and services from that office be available in both English and French.[14]

Section 23, Minority Language Educational Rights, was more controversial and gave rise to much opposition in Quebec where language policy at the time was orientated towards encouraging language transfer to French via the schools (see discussion on language policy in Quebec in Chapter 3). Provisions one and two of section 23 are as follows:

23 (1) Citizens of Canada

(a)   whose first language learned and still understood is that of the English or French linguistic minority population of the province in which they reside or

(b)   who have received their primary school instruction in Canada in English or French and reside in a province where the language in which they received that instruction is the language of the English or French linguistic minority population of the province, have the right to have their children receive primary and secondary school instruction in that language in that province.

(2) Citizens of Canada of whom any child has received or is receiving primary or secondary school instruction in English or French in Canada, have the right to have all their children receive primary and secondary instruction in the same language.

These rights are tempered by Section 3, which requires that certain conditions be met, i.e., that the numbers of qualifying children be

13   The Canadian Charter provisions on linguistic duality in Parliament and in the Courts have their origin in section 133 of the Constitution Act 1867 (Canada, 1867), discussed in Chapter 1.

14   Subsections of sections 16 to 20 make parallel provisions for the status of the official languages in New Brunswick.

sufficient to warrant provision from public funds.[15] Despite the guarantees given by the Canadian Charter, some parents seeking to avail of their rights have had to pursue the issue as far as the Supreme Court of Canada. In a long drawn out case taken by Franco-Albertan parents during the 1980s (which became known as the Mahé case) the Supreme Court of Canada held, in 1990, that official language minorities have a constitutional right to active participation, in all provinces of Canada, in the management of their children's schools.[16] A case was also taken in Prince Edward Island, the Arsenault-Cameron case, with a similar result.[17] A recent example (2003) is the Doucet-Boudreau case in which the applicants, francophone parents and the *Fédération des parents acadiens de la Nouvelle-Écosse* (Federation of Acadian Parents of Nova Scotia), had sought the provision of high school facilities in French in five municipalities from the Department of Education of Nova Scotia and the *Conseil scolaire acadien provincial* (Acadian Provincial School Board). The Supreme Court of Nova Scotia found in their favour, but the province appealed, and the Nova Scotia Court of Appeal reversed the judgment. However, the Supreme Court of Canada found in favour of the applicants, stating that when rights guaranteed by the Canadian Charter are violated the courts must uphold those rights.[18]

15   'The right of citizens of Canada under subsections (1) and (2) to have their children receive primary and secondary school instruction in the language of the English or French linguistic minority population of a province
(a) applies wherever in the province the number of children of citizens who have such a right is sufficient to warrant the provision to them out of public funds of minority language instruction; and
(b) includes, where the number of those children so warrants, the right to have them receive that instruction in minority language educational facilities provided out of public funds.' (Section 23 (3))
16   Mahé v. Alberta, 1990, S.C.R. 342.
17   Arsenault-Cameron et al. v. Prince Edward Island, 2000, 1 S.C.R. 3.
18   The Commissioner of Official Languages describes this judgment as 'historic'. For further commentary from the Commissioner's perspective see Canada. Commissioner of Official Languages (2003c).

The Official Languages Act 1988

In 1988, the federal government passed a second Official Languages Act, which updated and strengthened the 1969 Act and took into account developments that had taken place since then, in particular those resulting from the Canadian Charter. The main aims of the Act are to ensure that English and French are respected as the two official languages of Canada and that they have equal rights and status in federal institutions. Among other provisions, the Act:

- guarantees services in English and French where there is significant demand[19] [...]
- guarantees federal employees the right to work in the official language of their choice in certain regions;[20]
- aims at ensuring equitable opportunities for employment and advancement for English-speaking and French-speaking Canadians in federal institutions;
- aims to ensure that the Public Service is representative of the two official language groups;
- seeks to enhance the vitality of the English-speaking and French-speaking minority communities and to advance the status of English and French in Canadian society. (Canada. Commissioner of Official Languages, 2000: 2)

The Act also clarified the role of the Commissioner of Official Languages, for example, by allowing the Commissioner to seek a court remedy (under certain conditions) and to intervene in court proceedings concerning official languages.[21] In accordance with section 66 of the Act, the Commissioner submits an Annual Report to Parliament, but may also submit a special report at any time on any urgent matter arising. The Annual Reports of the Commissioner

---

19   Regulations concerning the definition of what constitutes 'significant demand' were adopted in January 1992 (Canada. Department of Justice, 1992).

20   Designated bilingual regions include, in addition to the NCR, parts of Eastern and Northern Ontario, the Montreal region, parts of Western Quebec, the Gaspé area and the Eastern Townships, and New Brunswick. (See Canada. Commissioner of Official Languages, 2004b).

21   The Commissioner intervened in the Doucet-Boudreau case discussed above.

provide detailed information on the operation of the Act,+[22] identifying specific examples of failure to comply with the act as well as giving awards and credit for good performance where warranted. Given the detailed picture they give of the reality of the situation, the Annual Reports are an invaluable source of 'real world' data, often providing a corrective to the idealised impression created by documents and statements of official policy. The Commissioner does not hesitate to identify cases where lip service is paid to the policy of bilingualism but the reality falls somewhat short of the stated aspirations. Her Annual Report of 1999–2000 was particularly hard-hitting in its criticism of what it identified as the federal government's failure to live up to its obligations under the Act. Under the heading 'An unacceptable situation', the Commissioner criticises the government unequivocally for its failures in the context of official languages:

> How can it be that the Office of the Commissioner must, year after year, present the government with a lengthy list of shortcomings identified in the implementation of this policy? How can it be that many government institutions are still characterised by an at best passive, if not defensive, attitude with regard to their obligations, and that they all too often take action only in response to court injunctions or threats of court remedy? [...] The lack of overall government commitment to implementation of the act is distressing. Implementation of the Act is not the responsibility of the Office of the Commissioner of Official Languages, but very much the government's responsibility. (Canada. Commissioner of Official Languages, 2000: 8)

Consequently, the Commissioner announced that henceforth her Office would be expanding and diversifying its modes of action. While continuing its work on investigation of complaints, it would put further emphasis on change by, for example, engaging in educational activities targeting young people especially, conducting studies, assisting with developing action plans and, in particular, by working towards transforming public service culture. The Commissioner calls on the government to provide effective political and administrative leadership (see quotation above) and stresses that she will not hesitate to use the various remedies at her disposal.

---

22   Dyane Adam's most recent (and final) Annual Report was submitted to Parliament in May 2006.

Federal language policy into the twenty-first century

The Action Plan for Official Languages

The Federal Government regularly reiterates its commitment to linguistic duality, often in the context of the Speech from the Throne at the opening of a new session of Parliament. Statements like 'Linguistic duality is at the heart of our identity' have become a recurring theme in the speeches (see Speeches from the Throne of 30 January 2001, 30 September 2002 and 2 February 2004).[23] Following the 1999–2000 Annual Report of the Commissioner of Official languages, the government of Jean Chrétien gave commitments to promote the linguistic duality of Canada, appointing a Minister Responsible for Official Languages, Stéphane Dion, President of the Queen's Privy Council and Minister of Intergovernmental Affairs, in April 2001. After two years of consultation with the federal administration, provincial and territorial governments and various minority official language groups, the Federal Government announced, in March 2003, a five-year *Action Plan for Official Languages* (Canada. Privy Council, 2003) intended to cover the period 2003 to 2008. In the plan, specific reference is made to the Commissioner's earlier criticisms (in her 1999–2000 Annual Report) and to the fact that progress since then had been commented upon favourably in her latest report. As well as insisting on the historical and cultural dimensions of linguistic duality, the plan draws attention to the substantial 'competitive edge' which Canadians have by virtue of their access to 'two of the most vital international languages' and to the fact that this represents 'an asset for labour markets and enhances mobility of individuals' (Canada. Privy Council, 2003: 2). The plan also provides a framework for accountability and coordination (see Annex A).

The *Action Plan for Official Languages* is an ambitious one, promising progress on three prioritised fronts: Education, Community

---

23   See Commissioner of Official Languages (2004a), for relevant excerpts from previous Speeches.

Development and the Public Service, with a total financial commitment of $751.3.[24] The government promises to give additional support to second language education, with the stated objective of more than doubling the number of bilingual young Canadians within ten years. The plan also addresses minority language education, with the aim that 'Within 10 years, the proportion of eligible students who attend French-language educational institutions will rise from 68% to 80%' (Canada. Privy Council, 2003: 61). Under the heading of Community Development for francophone and anglophone minorities, the government commits itself to further investment in the areas of health, early childhood development and justice. The plan for the federal public service is based on the premise that: 'The federal government cannot play a leadership role if it does not lead by example' (Canada. Privy Council, 2003: 9). The government renews its commitment to promoting the official languages in the public service, by such measures as improving language training and imposing higher expectations on levels of bilingualism among federal employees, with a view to creating an 'exemplary public service in the area of languages' (Canada. Privy Council, 2003: 53).

The objectives of the *Action Plan for Official Languages* would indeed, if achieved, be impressive. However, they may not be entirely realistic, for a number of reasons. The doubling of the numbers of bilingual young Canadians, a key goal of the plan, is dependent on the co-operation of the provinces if it is to become a reality. In times of budgetary cuts, it may be difficult to avoid money intended for second language education being channelled in other directions. The Commissioner of Official Languages expresses reservations about the government's intentions. In her Annual Report 2002–2003, she identifies a number of areas which have been neglected including:

– arts and culture;
– the bilingual status of the national capital; and
– the promotion of linguistic duality on the international scene.
(Canada. Commissioner of Official Languages, 2003b: 28)

---

24   Annex B of the Action Plan gives a breakdown of the financial commitments involved (Canada. Privy Council, 2003: 73–5).

She also suggests that greater emphasis could have been put on the development of bilingualism in the Public Service. In February 2004, almost a year after the plan was announced, she 'regrets the lack of a concrete commitment to implement the *Action Plan for Official Languages*' and does not see it as a 'panacea' (Commissioner of Official Languages, 2004a). In her report for 2004–2005, the Commissioner strikes a more positive note when she acknowledges 'a number of breakthroughs' in Departments such as Justice, Health, Citizenship and Immigration and Industry, though she criticises the government's 'significant delays' and 'major weaknesses' in some areas, notably the two major educational objectives, for which Canadian Heritage has responsibility (Canada. Commissioner of Official Languages, 2005b: 4–5).

The Commissioner's most recent report, for the period 2005–2006, acknowledges the further progress made on the Action Plan since her previous Annual Report, though she points to other measures which she believes are needed to continue the momentum, in particular the need to update the 1992 Regulations governing the Official Languages Act. These, she suggests, were 'developed to meet the needs of a bygone era [and] are no longer relevant and need to be modernized' (Canada. Commissioner of official languages, 2006: 25). The Commissioner's comments on the Action Plan specifically, and also on government policy and practice more generally, provide vital evidence for any assessment of the progress or otherwise of public policy, as they provide clear evidence of the linguistic reality of official languages across Canada, along with detailed analysis of trends and, in the context of her mandate, a proactive approach to the promotion of linguistic duality.

Amendment of the Official Languages Act: Bill S–3

In November 2005, the government strengthened its commitment to linguistic duality by adopting Bill S–3, amending the Official Languages Act. The effect of this Bill is that it imposes new obligations on all federal institutions.[25]

> These institutions must better equip stakeholders and work to enhance the vitality of official languages minority communities. Federal institutions must also be more active in promoting English and French within Canadian society. (Canada. Commissioner of Official Languages, 2006: i)

The amendments in question were made to Part VII of the Act, in particular Section 41, which deals with enhancing the vitality of minority language communities. Previously, governments had been able to exploit a certain amount of ambiguity in the Act and thereby minimise their obligations, interpreting them as vague political commitments which could be ignored, rather than as requirements for action. This change means that any possible ambiguity has been removed and federal institutions have clear responsibilities 'to ensure that positive measures are taken for the implementation of the commitments' (section 41.2). A further reinforcement of the Act by Bill S–3 is the amendment to section 77, to which Part VII has been added, with the effect that recourse to a Court remedy is now possible in the event of a violation of the Act.

---

25 The term 'federal institutions' refers to government departments, agencies, Crown corporations and organizations which are subject to the Official Languages Act.

Conclusion

The changes to the Official Languages Act indicate significant progress in the direction of promoting linguistic duality and enhancing the vitality of minority language communities. At the very least a new instrument has been put in place which imposes obligations on federal institutions and there is a more robust way of ensuring compliance with the provisions of the Act. It remains to be seen whether the political will exists to achieve the ambitious goals set out in the Action Plan for Official Languages or whether financial or other constraints will consign them largely to the dustbin of history. The year 2013 will be the fiftieth anniversary of the establishment of the historic Royal Commission on Bilingualism and Biculturalism and by then it will be abundantly clear whether or not the goals of the Action Plan have been achieved, whether minority language communities have enjoyed renewed vitality and indeed whether the principle of linguistic duality remains a key defining feature of Canadian society and 'Canadian-ness' into the second decade of the twenty-first century.

Key Dates

1963–70	Royal Commission on Bilingualism and Biculturalism
1969	Official Languages Act
1982	Canadian Charter of Rights and Freedoms
1984	Supreme Court judgment on language of instruction
1988	Official Languages Act
1988	Supreme Court judgment (Ford) on signage
2003	Action Plan for Official Languages
2005	Supreme Court judgments on language of instruction in Quebec

3 Language policy and language planning at the Provincial level: Quebec

Introduction

The province of Quebec underwent great social transformation during the decades of the 1960s and 1970s accompanied by an increase in nationalist and separatist sentiments. The French language had always been a central feature of the distinctive identity of French-speaking Canadians. The role of language became even more important in Quebec with the advent of the more strongly legislative approach to language policy which came to the fore during the 1960s and 1970s, and which had as its objective the promotion of French as the primary language of education and work. Though the *Loi Lavergne* had been passed in 1910 (making travel tickets obligatorily bilingual), it was an isolated measure rather than an element of a comprehensive policy. In 1961 a more concerted approach to language policy and planning was evident in the setting up of the *Office de la langue française*, which was created by the *Loi instituant le ministère des Affaires culturelles*, sanctioned on 24 March. In 1967, the use of French was made obligatory on the labelling of agricultural products.[1] Some of these initiatives took place as the federal Royal Commission on Bilingualism and Biculturalism, set up in 1963, was carrying on its work and revealing many of the inequalities which characterised the lives of Francophones, by contrast with Anglophones, even in Quebec.

---

1   The requirement that all products be labelled in French was included subsequently in article 51 of the *Charte de la langue française* (1977), (see Quebec, 2003: 11). Similarly, the provision on bilingual travel tickets was incorporated in article 30 (see Quebec, 2003: 6).

Language policy before 1977

The government of Quebec took the initiative, in December 1968, of setting up its own Commission, the Gendron Commission, to enquire into the status of French in Quebec. The Commission reported in 1973 and gave a very similar picture to that noted by the Royal Commission at the federal level. Its findings included the prevalence of English at work in Quebec, as well as marked inequalities in the status and salary levels of Francophones. The Commission recommended as follows:

> In America, French is a fringe language. As such, its use is restricted even in areas where it is spoken by a majority of the population. This situation requires a clear policy: French can survive and flourish on the North American continent only with a maximum of opportunity and protection throughout Québec; and this can be accomplished only by making it a useful communication instrument for all people of this area. [...]
>
> This government action should aim at establishing French as the common language of Québecers by making it useful and necessary for everyone in work communication. (Gendron, 1973: 151–2)

However, the government did not wait for the recommendations of the Gendron Commission before taking action. Education became the battleground for controversial language issues in the late 1960s. Violent demonstrations took place when the School Board of St-Léonard (Montreal) decided, in 1969, to impose instruction in French on immigrant children and the government introduced Bill 63, *Loi pour promouvoir la langue française au Québec*, which was adopted on 20 November 1969. The Bill made the teaching of French obligatory in the anglophone school sector, mentioned for the first time the objective of making French the language of work and that French should have priority in public signage. The Bill provoked much opposition and political controversy among the francophone population, who thought it was too weak, since, in effect, it allowed parents to choose whether their children would be educated in English or

French.[2] A group called *Le Front commun du Québec français* was formed to oppose some provisions of the Bill, in particular, the choice of English or French instruction. The group also demanded that the National Assembly proclaim French monolingualism.[3]

The events of the time (the St-Léonard language riot and Bill 63) were depicted in various literary productions, such as the play by Françoise Loranger, entitled *Medium Saignant*, (Loranger, 1970) performed in January 1970. In the two-act play, Loranger portrays very strikingly the fear which gave rise to the language laws of Quebec. The play had a strong impact, given the situation of political uncertainty and fear which existed in Quebec at the time. Indeed, the October Crisis was only some months away. Another literary event which caught the imagination of *Québécois* by its representation of their experience at the time was the performance, in March 1970, of a poem by Michèle Lalonde entitled *Speak White* (Lalonde, 1974). The poem has since become one of the best known texts of Quebec poetry.[4]

However rudimentary and controversial Bill 63 was, it represented a step in the direction of introducing further legislative measures. In 1970 a law was passed which required those seeking a permit to practise a profession to have an appropriate knowledge of French.[5] Bill 63 was eventually repealed and the Quebec Liberal Government of Robert Bourassa replaced it in July 1974 with Bill 22, which went much further by declaring that French was the official

---

2   The *Archives télé de Radio-Canada* contain a video-clip which illustrates the negative reaction among Francophones to Bill 63: 'La loi 63 soulève l'ire des francophones', available at http://archives.radio-canada.ca/IDC-0-17-1300-7521/politique_economie/loi_101/clip4.

3   See Provost, Gilles, 'Un Front commun du Québec français organise la résistance contre le bill 63', *Le Devoir*, 27 October 1969.

4   Michèle Lalonde subsequently published *Défense et illustration de la langue québécoise*, a collection of her texts dealing with Quebec identity.

5   This requirement was incorporated into the *Charte de la langue française*, as article 35: 'Les ordres professionels ne peuvent délivrer de permis qu'à des personnes ayant de la langue officielle une connaissance appropriée à l'exercice de leur profession.' (Quebec, 2003: 7) ('The professional corporations shall not issue permits except to persons whose knowledge of the official language is appropriate to the practice of their profession.')

language of Quebec (*Loi sur la langue officielle*). This Bill included several measures designed to improve the status of French not only at governmental level, but also in the areas of business and education. French would be the language of communication of the government of Quebec, but it would also be the language of business. Companies would have to undergo a process of francization[6] and commercial signage would be in French. Access to education in English was restricted. While parents would still have free choice between English and French schools, those wishing to attend English schools would have to prove sufficient competence in English, and that competence was to be ascertained by a language test. The test results would determine whether the child enrolled at an English or French school. In some senses, Bill 22 left opposing groups equally dissatisfied, at both extremes of the debate. The fact that their children's English had to be tested before they could attend English schools enraged anglophone parents. For the more nationalist among Quebecers, the bill did not go far enough in the direction of a monolingual Quebec. The enactment of the Charter of the French language in 1977 represented a tougher stance on many fronts, including the limitation of access to education in English.

6   The term 'francization' is the translation of the French term 'francisation', recommended by *Le Nouveau Grand dictionnaire terminologique,* which is available for consultation online at www.olf.gouv.ca/resources/gdt_bdl.html. The definition given in this dictionary is: 'Processus qui vise la généralisation de l'utilisation du français notamment dans les communications internes, les communications avec le public, l'affichage et la publicité.' ('A process which has the objective of generalising the use of French particularly in internal communications, communications with the public, signage and advertising.')

The *Charte de la langue française*, 1977

The defeat of Bourassa's Quebec Liberals and the election of René Lévesque's *Parti Québécois* (PQ) government on 15 November 1976 signalled a new period of radical language policy change. A new language law was high on the agenda of the *PQ* and it passed a momentous piece of language legislation on 26 August 1977, the *Charte de la langue française* ('Quebec Charter'), or Bill 101, as it is commonly known. This Bill represented the end result of the debate which had produced Bill 63 in 1969 and Bill 22 in 1974. It was a historic turning point in the official promotion of monolingualism in Quebec, a highly significant declaration of intent with regard to the status and development of French in the province. The intrinsic connection between the language and the identity of Quebecers was made very explicit indeed.

The Preamble to the Quebec Charter set out very clearly its rationale and intentions:

> Langue distinctive d'un peuple majoritairement francophone, la langue française permet au people québécois d'exprimer son identité.
> L'Assemblée nationale [...] est donc résolue à faire du français la langue de l'État et de la Loi aussi bien que la langue normale et habituelle du travail, de l'enseignement, des communications, du commerce et des affaires.[7] (Quebec, 2003: 1)

The emphasis was on the rights of Quebecers in relation to use of the French language in various contexts. The Quebec Charter went on to develop in detail each individual's 'Fundamental Language Rights', such as the right of every person to communicate in French with such

---

7   'The French language, the distinctive language of a people that is in the majority French-speaking, is the instrument by which that people has articulated its identity;
    The National Assembly of Quebec [...] is resolved therefore to make of French the language of Government and the Law, as well as the normal and everyday language of work, instruction, communication, commerce and business.' (This and other English translations of the text of the Quebec Charter are quoted from the *Office québécois de la langue française* website.)

bodies as the civil administration, the health and social services, public utility firms and all business firms. Workers were given the right to carry out their professional activities in French. Consumers had the right to be served in French. Everyone eligible for instruction had the right to receive it in French.

As well as guaranteeing French language rights, the Quebec Charter also dealt with the other side of the coin, i.e., the restriction of English language rights. It imposed:

- The exclusive use of French in public signage and commercial advertising
- The restriction of access to schooling in English to children one of whose parents received their elementary education in English in Quebec
- The extension of francization programmes to businesses employing fifty people or more.

The Quebec Charter also created mechanisms for ensuring the application of the law, namely the *Conseil de la langue française* and the *Commission de surveillance de la langue française*, and further defined the role of the *Office de la langue française*, which had been set up in 1961. A *Commission de toponymie* was also instituted and attached to the *Office de la langue française*, with the function of advising on place names. The roles, functions, powers and titles of some of these organisations have been amended on various occasions since the adoption of the Quebec Charter in 1977.[8] For example, the *Commission de protection de la langue française* replaced the *Commission de surveillance de la langue française* in 1983, was in turn disbanded by Bill 86 in 1993, and re-established by Bill 40 in 1997. In 2002, Bill 104 fused the *Commission de protection de la langue française* with the *Office de la langue française*, to form the new *Office québécois de la langue française* (OQLF). Also in 2002, the *Conseil de la langue française* was renamed as the *Conseil supérieur de la langue française* (CSLF). These two bodies are currently the two

8   The Quebec Charter was amended substantially by Bill 57 (1983), Bill 178 (1988), Bill 86 (1993), Bill 40 (1997) and Bill 104 (2002).

organisations charged with overseeing the application, and in the case of the OQLF, the levying of sanctions against those who do not comply with the provisions of the Quebec Charter. The enforcement role which the Quebec Charter assigned to the organisations set up by it has provoked much criticism and resulted in the characterisation of these organisations as 'linguistic police'.

The aftermath of the *Charte de la langue française*

The astringency of the new rules, in particular the restrictions with regard to public signage and instruction through English provoked extremely strong reaction particularly in the anglophone community in Quebec, with ripples throughout the rest of Canada. Quebec Anglophones were shocked to find that they were now reduced to minority status, having previously seen themselves as part of the national linguistic majority.[9] A stream of Anglophones took the decision to leave the province, thus significantly reducing the proportion of Anglophones. Some of those who stayed chose the legal route, taking court cases to defend and promote their rights, particularly on the issues of access to education and signage. With the adoption by the federal government of the Canadian Charter in 1982, some clauses of the Quebec Charter were in conflict with the provisions of the Canadian Charter and cases were taken as far as the Supreme Court of Canada for judgment, especially in the areas of language of instruction and public signage and commercial advertising.

---

9   See Caldwell (2002) and Chambers (2000) for detailed discussion of the reaction of Quebec anglophones to the Quebec Charter and other legislative instruments.

The language of instruction

On the issue of language of instruction, the Supreme Court of Canada found, on 26 July 1984, that article 73 of the Quebec Charter, which allowed only the children of a parent who had received the major part of his or her elementary education in English in Quebec to attend an English school, was incompatible with the provisions of article 23 of the Canadian Charter.[10] As a result, article 73 of the Quebec Charter had to be changed to include those who had received the major part of their elementary education in English elsewhere in Canada. Section 73 of the Quebec Charter, as amended, now reads:

> Peuvent recevoir l'enseignement en anglais, à la demande de l'un de leurs parents:
> (1) les enfants dont le père ou la mère est citoyen canadien et a reçu un enseignement primaire en anglais au Canada, pourvu que cet enseignement constitue la majeure partie de l'enseignement primaire reçu au Canada. [...]
> (2) les enfants dont le père ou la mère est citoyen canadien et qui ont reçu ou reçoivent un enseignement primaire ou secondaire en anglais au Canada, de même que leurs frères et sœurs, pourvu que cet enseignement constitue la majeure partie de l'enseignement primaire ou secondaire reçu au Canada; (Quebec, 2003: 14)[11]

Further detail is provided on what constitutes recognised education in English for the purposes of the Quebec Charter; notably, education in private schools is not recognised.

---

10   A.G. of Quebec v. Quebec Protestant School Boards (1984) 2 R.C.S. 66.

11   'The following children, at the request of one of their parents, may receive instruction in English;
(1) a child whose father or mother is a Canadian citizen and received elementary instruction in English in Canada, provided that that instruction constitutes the major part of the elementary instruction he or she received in Canada;
(2) a child whose father or mother is a Canadian citizen and who has received or is receiving elementary or secondary instruction in English in Canada, and the brothers and sisters of that child, provided that that instruction constitutes the major part of the elementary or secondary instruction received by the child in Canada.'

The issue of access to education in English remains contentious. On 31 March 2005, the Supreme Court of Canada delivered judgments on challenges to the Quebec Charter brought by Quebec francophone and allophone[12] parents, argued on their behalf by the lawyer Brent Tyler, ex-President of the Alliance Quebec English rights lobby group. In one of the cases, a parent, Edwige Casimir,[13] had been refused a certificate of eligibility for her daughter Shanning to attend English school, when the family moved from Ontario to Quebec, on the grounds that she had not received the major part of her education in English in Canada (as required by s.73(2) of the Quebec Charter, quoted above).[14] In fact, the child had attended a fifty per cent French immersion programme in an anglophone school. The Quebec Superior Court dismissed the case in 2000 and this decision was upheld by the Court of Appeal. If the case were successful at the Supreme Court, it would have far-reaching implications for Quebec, invalidating a central provision of the Quebec Charter. Such a decision would allow all parents in Quebec, whatever their origin or first language, to have freedom of choice with regard to the language of instruction of their children.[15] In the event, the Supreme Court did not overturn the Quebec ruling, holding that the 'major part' criterion was constitutional. However, it did uphold the appeal in part, finding that the interpretation of 'major part' should not be strictly quantitative, but should involve a qualitative assessment.

12 The term 'Allophone' refers to someone whose first language is neither English nor French.
13 Edwige Casimir v. Attorney General of Quebec, et al. (Qc) 29297) 2005 SCC 14. For the full text of the judgment, see the website of the Supreme Court of Canada at www.scc-csc.gc.ca/information/hearings/winter/winter_e.asp.
14 For further details of the case, see the website of the Supreme Court of Canada at www.scc-csc.gc.ca/information/hearings/winter/winter_e.asp (no. 29299).
15 The Commissioner of Official Languages intervened in the Casimir case. See the Commissioner's website for the text of her intervention at www.ocol-clo.gc.ca/archives/interventions/2004–02–10_casimir_e.htm. For newspaper reports on the issue see 'La loi 101 devant la Cour suprême', *La Presse*, 22 mars 2004, 'Powder keg language cases reach top court', *The Gazette*, 23 March 2004, 'Quebec parents fight language laws', *The Ottawa Citizen*, 23 March 2004.

The qualitative assessment will determine if a significant part, though not necessarily the majority, of the child's instruction, considered cumulatively, was in the minority language. [...] To purposefully assess the requirement for participation in s.23(2), therefore, all the circumstances of the child must be considered including the time spent in each programme, at what stage of education the choice of language instruction was made, what programs were or were not available, and whether learning disabilities or other difficulties exist. The relevance of each factor will vary with the facts of each case and other factors may also arise depending on the circumstances of the particular child and his or her educational experience.[16]

This judgment, therefore, while not requiring a change in the letter of the law, affects significantly the interpretation and application of the Quebec Charter in practice.

The second case on which the Supreme Court handed down a judgment was the Gosselin case,[17] taken by a group of eight franco-phone families, who wanted to send their children to English schools. This appeal was rejected, on the grounds that their rights under Section 23 of the Canadian Charter (protecting minority language rights) were not contravened, as they were members of the franco-phone majority in Quebec. The effect of this judgment is that the provisions of the Quebec Charter on access to English schools remain valid.[18]

A wide range of reactions to the judgments was reported in the Quebec and Canadian media on the following day, 1 April 2005.[19] Some differences of interpretation were apparent, even in francophone newspapers, in that some commentators hailed the fact that the Quebec Charter had passed the Supreme Court test, while others referred to a breach in the law:

---

16   For the full text of the Supreme Court judgment, see www.lexum.umontreal. ca/csc-scc/en/bul/2005/05-04-01-bul.wpd.html.

17   Roger Gosselin et al. v. Attorney General of Quebec, et al. (Qc) (29298) SCC 15.

18   A third judgment (not discussed here), reaffirmed the right of the Administra-tive Tribunal of Quebec to hear claims for minority language instruction.

19   For detailed discussion of media reaction, see Conrick (2005a).

'La loi 101 passe le test suprême', Mylène Moisan in *Le Soleil* (Quebec)
'Une brèche dans la loi 101', Sylvain Larocque in *Le Devoir* (Ottawa-Hull)

Across Canada, several articles referred to the change in the position of Anglophones and Allophones, while the position of francophones remained the same. Francophones were described as being 'rebuffed' (Jim Brown, *Winnipeg Free Press*, 1 April 2005) and treated 'like second class citizens' (Diane Francis, *The National Post*, 31 March 2005) while a letter to the editor of *The Montreal Gazette* (2 April 2005) suggested that the 'ruling enslaves francophones'. Political reaction from the Quebec government was positive, as was to be expected, with Intergovernmental Affairs Minister Benoît Pelletier expressing relief that the wording of the law did not have to be changed: 'Nous sommes soulagés. Si la loi avait été déclarée invalide, nous aurions eu un problème important à résoudre.'[20]

In essence, the Supreme Court judgment in the case of non-francophones has changed an important aspect of the interpretation of the Quebec Charter, as it applies to language of instruction, despite the fact that the text does not have to be amended. The need to make a qualitative judgment in each case removes the relative certainty of the numerical test of 'major part', replacing it with a more subjective assessment of what constitutes a 'significant part'. This amounts to a relaxation of the law, even if the letter of the law remains unchanged. Even though a linguistic crisis has been averted, it is clear from media reaction that debate on access to instruction in English is likely to continue.

Public signage and commercial advertising

Another area in which there has been conflict between Quebec provincial law and the Canadian Charter is the area of public signage and commercial advertising. In 1988, in the Ford judgment, the Supreme Court found that the prohibition of any language other than French on

---

20   The press conference at which this remark was made was reported widely, for example by Robert Dutrisac in *Le Devoir*, 1 April 2005. ('If the law had been declared invalid, we would have had a major problem to resolve.')

public and commercial signs was not consistent with freedom of expression, as guaranteed by the Canadian Charter. The Premier of Quebec, Robert Bourassa, in order to retrieve the situation, and in the face of angry demonstrations by supporters of Bill 101, introduced Bill 178, invoking the 'notwithstanding' clause of the Canadian Charter, thus allowing Quebec a derogation from its provisions for five years.[21] Bill 178 stipulated that commercial signage had to be in French on external signs, but English could be used in internal signs, provided that French was '*nettement prédominant*' (markedly predominant).[22] Some years later, the Premier of Ontario, David Peterson commented that resorting to the 'notwithstanding' clause put 'a stake through the heart of the Meech Lake Accord'. Obviously, the language policy enshrined in Bill 101, and consequent efforts to defend it, had much wider political rather than purely linguistic ramifications. In 1993, Bourassa introduced Bill 86, which attenuated the original provisions considerably by allowing English on outdoor commercial signage, provided that French was clearly predominant.

Despite the relaxation of the strictures of the Quebec Charter which Bill 86 constituted, litigants continue to contest the issue of English in commercial signage. An example of a lengthy and high-profile case is that taken by Gwen Simpson and Wally Hoffman, the owners of a small antique shop near Montreal called the 'Lyon and the Walrus', who contested a fine of $500 imposed on them because the lettering on the sign outside their premises was the same size in English and French (an infringement of Article 58). The case progressed through the Quebec courts and was appealed to the Supreme Court of

21 The 'notwithstanding' clause refers to section 33 (1) of the Canadian Charter: 'Parliament or the legislature of a province may expressly declare in an Act of Parliament or of the legislature, as the case may be, that the Act or a provision thereof shall operate notwithstanding a provision included in section 2 or sections 7 to 15 of this Charter.' Section 33. (3) allows for such a declaration to remain in force for up to five years.

22 The definition of what the phrase 'markedly predominant' means in practice for the purposes of the Quebec Charter is defined by a regulation published in the *Gazette officielle du Québec*, along with other regulations on matters of detail regarding the provisions of the Quebec Charter. (These regulations are available on the OQLF website.)

Canada, which ruled in December 2002 that it would not hear the couple's appeal and so Quebec's law on signage remains valid, i.e., French must be predominant in commercial signage. This case was supported by the group Alliance Quebec, with Brent Tyler, then President of the group, saying that he would continue to pursue the issue to the United Nations.[23] Such cases tend to be reported widely in the Canadian media, both francophone and anglophone, suggesting that commercial signage remains an issue of strong public interest.[24] However, the decision of the Supreme Court to uphold Quebec's position should bring the matter to a close from a legal point of view.

Another example of the controversy which surrounds the commercial signage issue was provided by Jacques Villeneuve, the Formula 1 racing driver, when he opened a restaurant in downtown Montreal in June 2001, which he called 'Newtown', the translation of his surname and his nickname on the racing circuit. The name 'Newtown' is a registered trademark and therefore exempt from the signage laws, but nonetheless, it gave rise to several complaints to the *Office de la langue française*. A more sinister situation occurred the previous year (October 2000), when three Second Cup cafés in the Plateau Mont-Royal area of Montreal were firebombed by the *Brigade d'autodéfense du français* (French Self-Defence Brigade), as part of a campaign against businesses with English names.[25]

---

23 See 'La Croisade de Brent Tyler contre la Loi 101 – après un échec en Cour suprême, les Nations Unies', *Le Devoir*, (Montreal), 13 December 2002. He has said more recently (2005) that he will also pursue the issue of access to instruction in English to the UN.

24 See for example an article in the Toronto daily newspaper, *The Globe and Mail*, entitled 'Supreme Court rejects review of Quebec sign law – Antique shop loses bid to overturn rule that French must predominate on commercial signs', 12 December 2002. See also an article in the Montreal daily newspaper, *La Presse*, entitled 'Prédominance du français. Fin d'une saga sur l'affichage – La Cour suprême du Canada refuse d'entendre l'appel d'un commerçant de Lac-Brôme, mettant ainsi fin à une longue saga judiciaire sur la langue d'affichage au Québec', 12 December 2002.

25 Rhéal Mathieu, a former member of the Front de libération du Québec (FLQ), the group involved in the October crisis of 1970, was charged with the offences. See, for example, the following reports: 'Bouchard condamne les attentats

Language policy agencies

Among the organisations involved in the implementation of language policy in Quebec are currently: the *Conseil supérieur de la langue française* (CSLF), the *Commission de toponymie du Québec*, the *Office québécois de la langue française* (OQLF) (all three created and regulated by the Quebec Charter) and the *Secrétariat à la politique linguistique*.

Conseil supérieur de la langue française

The role of the CSLF is to advise the Minister responsible for the application of the Quebec Charter on all matters related to the French language in Quebec. The mission of the CSLF is defined as follows by Article 187 of the Quebec Charter:

> 187.
> Le Conseil a pour mission de conseiller le minister responsable de l'application de la présente loi sur toute question relative à la langue française au Québec.
> À ce titre, le Conseil:
> 1. donne son avis au ministre sur toute question que celui-ci lui soumet;
> 2. saisit le ministre de toute question qui, selon lui, appelle l'attention du gouvernement.[26]

To further this end, the CSLF carries out various studies and research projects on issues of language policy and planning. Some recent studies focused on an issue of continued concern, 'la qualité de la langue', examining the quality of language used by the authors of 4,000 emails, by pre-school teachers and by newscasters on a variety

contre Second Cup', *La Tribune*, 7 October 2000, 'Attentats contre Second Cup à Montréal: Au nom de la langue', *Le Soleil*, 7 October 2000.

26   'The mission of the Conseil is to advise the Minister responsible for the administration of this Act on any matter relating to the French language in Québec. In that capacity, the Conseil shall advise the Minister on any matter the Minister submits to it; bring to the Minister's attention any matter which, in its opinion, requires the attention of the Government.'

of radio channels. The CSLF also publishes three times a year a newsletter, the *Bulletin du Conseil de la langue française*, which informs the public on language-related matters. Many of the CSLF documents are published on its website and are thus available to a wide audience. Another activity of the CSLF is the awarding of prizes in recognition of the contributions of individuals and organisations to the promotion of French, such as the *Prix du 3-juillet-1608*, which commemorates the foundation of Quebec by Samuel de Champlain, the *Prix Jules-Fournier*, awarded for the linguistic excellence of journalists in the print media, the *Prix Raymond-Charrette*, for the electronic media, and the *Ordre des francophones d'Amérique*,[27] awarded to people and organisations who have made a significant contribution to the development of the language and culture of 'l'Amérique française'.

Commission de toponymie du Québec

The objective of the *Commission de toponymie du Québec*, which is attached administratively to the OQLF, is to plan and manage all aspects of place names in Quebec. Its mandate is defined by Articles 122–128 of the *Charte*. Article 125 details the Commission's duties:

> 125. La commission doit:
> a) proposer au gouvernement les normes et les règles d'écriture à respecter dans la dénomination des lieux;
> b) procéder à l'inventaire et à la conservation des noms de lieux;
> c) établir et normaliser le terminologie géographique, en collaboration avec l'Office;
> d) officialiser les noms de lieux;
> e) diffuser la nomenclature géographique officielle du Québec;
> f) donner son avis au gouvernement sur toute question que celui-ci soumet en matière de toponymie.[28]

---

27 In 2006 seven awards were made in six categories: Quebec, Acadia, Ontario, the Canadian West, the Americas and Other Continents (See the Bulletin of the CSLF, 2004: 1–5, for details of the recipients).

28 'The Commission shall: (a) propose to the Government the standards and rules of spelling to be followed in place names; (b) catalogue and preserve place

As well as advising the government on establishing and standardising geographic terminology, it provides advice in the form of publications, such as the *Répertoire toponymique du Québec*, *Noms et Lieux du Québec: dictionnaire illustré* and TOPOS, a database of official Quebec place names, as well as a free personalized consultation service and a library service.

Office québécois de la langue française (OQLF)

Of all the agencies associated with language policy, planning and implementation in Quebec, the OQLF is probably the public body with the highest profile. It was created by the *Loi instituant le ministère des affaires culturelles*, on 24 March 1961.[29] Under the title *Office québécois de la langue française* (OQLF), its brief is currently defined by sections 159 to 177 of the *Charte*, which describe its mission and powers as follows:

> 159. L'Office définit et conduit la politique québécoise en matière d'officialisation linguistique, de terminologie ainsi que de francisation de l'Administration et des enterprises.
> Il est également chargé d'assurer le respect de la présente loi. [...]
> 161. L'Office veille à ce que le français soit la langue normale et habituelle du travail, des communications, du commerce et des affaires dans l'Administration et les enterprises. Il peut notamment prendre toute mesure appropriée pour assurer la promotion du français.
> Il aide à définir et à élaborer les programmes de francisation prévus par la présente loi et en suit l'application.[30]

names; (c) establish and standardize geographical terminology, in cooperation with the Office; (d) officialize place names; (e) publicize the official geographical nomenclature of Québec; (f) advise the Government on any question submitted by it to the Commission relating to toponymy.'

29 See Cholette (1993) for an account of the early history of the Office from 1961 to 1974.

30 '159. The Office is responsible for defining and conducting Québec policy on linguistic officialisation, terminology and the francization of the civil administration and enterprises. The Office is also responsible for ensuring compliance with this Act. [...]' 161. The Office shall see to it that French is the normal and everyday language of work, communication, commerce and

The OQLF engages in a range of activities pursuant to the provisions of the Quebec Charter. As well as defining and carrying out Quebec government policy on language, the OQLF provides many services to the general public, to the civil administration, to businesses and to researchers. These include a general information telephone service, an advisory service on francization for businesses with fifty or more employees, publications on terminology and a library service. Publications include *Le français au bureau* and a journal entitled *La revue d'aménagement linguistique*, as well as numerous booklets, brochures and posters on various areas of terminology.[31] In addition, the OQLF website offers free access to terminological and reference tools, in particular the *Nouveau Grand Dictionnaire terminologique*[32] and the *Banque de dépannage linguistique*.

One of the areas of activity of agencies involved in language policy which gives rise to public scrutiny and a considerable amount of criticism is the role of ensuring compliance with the Act. This role was attributed to the OQLF by the amendments made to the Quebec Charter on 1 October 2002 (Bill 104) and involves receiving, responding to and investigating complaints from the public and, if necessary, referring the complaint to the *Procureur général* (Attorney General), after which fines may be levied where violations are deemed to have occurred. The following are some examples of possible infringements of the provisions of the *Charte*:

business in the civil administration and in enterprises. The Office may, among other things, take any appropriate measure to promote French. The Office shall help define and develop the francization programmes provided for in this Act and monitor their application.'

31   See René (2001) for discussion of OQLF policy on the production and diffusion of terminology in French. Some of the areas which the author, then President of the OQLF, mentions as priorities are: information technology, health services, and cars. The current President is France Boucher.

32   Paquette (2006) points out that there were in the region of 68 million online consultations of the *Grand Dictionnaire* in 2005, and that the new (sixth) edition of *Le français au bureau* had sold 25,000 copies, from autumn 2005 to June 2006.

- A product with packaging or instructions which are not in French.
- A brochure or catalogue distributed in Quebec in a language other than French.
- A communication which is not in French, sent by an employer to all staff.
- Computer software offered only in a language other than French, when a French version exists.[33]

Efforts are made by the OQLF to inform people of their obligations and to encourage them to comply. Unless the situation is resolved at that stage, penalties which range between 250 and 700$ for a '*personne physique*' and 500 to 1400$ for a '*personne morale*'[34] may be imposed, for each offence (Article 205). Repeat offences attract higher penalties, 500–1,400$ and 1,000–7,000$ respectively. An analysis of the penalties for 2005 shows that they have been imposed mostly (almost 75%) for failure to observe the provisions of Articles 51 and 52 (labelling of commercial products, instruction leaflets, brochures, catalogues, etc.), though there have also been contraventions of other Articles, such as Article 41 (requirement to use French in communications to employees and in job advertisements), Article 58 (public signage and commercial advertising), Articles 139, 140 and 143 (francization programme) and Article 176 (failure to supply requested information or documents). Table 3.1 details fines imposed for the years 2001–2005.[35]

---

33   These examples are sourced from an information leaflet prepared by the OQLF, entitled *Comment faire respecter ses droits linguistiques*.
34   These terms are translated by the OQLF as 'a natural person' and 'a legal person' respectively.
35   The figures for 2006 were complete, at time of writing, up to 19 June 2006. The number of infractions is listed as 71.

Year	Total number	Range of fines
2005	154	250 – 5000 $
2004	131	250 – 5000 $
2003	123	250 – 4200 $
2002	181	250 – 1000 $
2001	103	250 – 1000 $

Table 3.1: Penalties imposed under the Charte de la langue française

The names of the companies are published, along with details of the infraction, date and amount of fines, on the OQLF website and include (for 2005): Bureau en Gros / The Business Depot Ltd., Canadian Tire, Électrolux Canada Corporation, Hôtel Radisson Laval, La Compagnie Walmart du Canada, Microbytes, Polo Ralph Lauren, Sir Winston Churchill Pub, Sony du Canada Ltée, Université McGill-Collège McDonald.

Secrétariat à la politique linguistique

The *Secrétariat à la politique linguistique* reports to the Minister responsible for the Quebec Charter and has the role of advising the Minister with regard to the implementation of the province's language policy. It is involved in coordinating work on amendments to language legislation and regulations. The *Secrétariat* also distributes information in the form of publications, brochures and access to databases, the *Réseau des corpus lexicaux québécois*, produced by the French-speaking universities, for linguists and all those interested in French in Quebec. It also awards the Prix Georges-Émile-Lapalme to honour the career of people who have made a distinguished contribution to the quality and promotion of spoken or written French in Quebec.

Conclusion

After more than forty years of relatively sustained interest in language policy in Canada and in Quebec in particular, some issues still remain unresolved. The tensions between federal and provincial perspectives and interests were evident especially during the 1970s and 80s in the enactment of major pieces of legislation such as the Canadian Charter of Rights and Freedoms and, in Quebec, the *Charte de la langue française*, both of which guaranteed (initially conflicting) language rights. The inequalities between French and English speakers identified by the Royal Commission on Bilingualism and Biculturalism in the 1960s have largely been addressed. Taking the example of the public service, the Commissioner of Official Languages reported in 2005 that it had become more representative of the presence of Francophones in Canada, as the proportion of French speakers in the public service (including the seven main federal agencies) had increased to 27% in 2004 from 21% in 1966 (Canada. Commissioner of Official Languages, 2005a: 49). This is not to suggest that the reality matches the ideal in all cases. Indeed, the Commissioner's Annual Reports indicate that much work remains to be done so that the progress towards bilingualism which has already been made may be sustained.

Quebec today is a vibrant society, increasingly looking outwards and to the future, rather than inwards and to the past. While many Quebecers – and even more so French-speakers outside Quebec – remain concerned about the survival of French in a vast anglophone country and continent, much progress has been made in promoting and establishing French as a viable, modern language, which possesses all the necessary resources to function in a more diverse world. Agencies like the OQLF have played a vital role in adapting the existing linguistic resources of the language by, for example, updating the lexis of French to enable its users to cope with such new social realities as information and other technologies and the need to modernise the language to take account of the changing role of women.[36] All of these activities have contributed to improving the status of French, not only within Canada, but internationally. Initiatives in language policy in Canada and Quebec have inspired other countries to follow suit. Two notable examples of the international impact of language policy measures are the *Loi Toubon* (1994) in France, which adopted some of the approaches evidenced by the Quebec Charter, and the enactment by Ireland of an Official Languages Act (2003) along the lines of the Canadian legislation.

The tone of many commentators on language in Quebec has changed from defensive to confident, from exclusive to inclusive. The report of the *Commission des États généraux sur la situation et la l'avenir de la langue française au Québec* (2001) takes a very positive line in expressing the desirability of leaving behind the old rivalries between French and English and moving forward towards a new, more inclusive, definition of Quebec identity based on the concept of Quebec citizenship, with French as the language of expression of that citizenship. The Commission's first recommendation is:

> Que la politique linguistique du Québec rompe définitivement avec l'approche historique canadienne qui divise l'identité québécoise suivant une ligne de partage ethnique, la canadienne-française et la canadienne-anglaise, pour lui substituer une approche civique qui fonde l'identité du peuple du Québec sur l'accueil et l'inclusion grâce à une langue commune, le français, et à une culture commune formée des apports de toutes ses composantes. (Québec. Commission des États généraux sur la situation et l'avenir de la langue française au Québec, 2001: 21)[37]

The Quebec Charter has been in existence for more than twenty five years. In that time, controversy has never been far away, especially when different linguistic groups felt that their rights were being threatened or infringed in some way. Many issues such as the use of

---

36 For discussion of the issue of the linguistic representation of women in French, see Conrick (2002a) and (2005b).

37 'That language policy in Quebec abandon definitively the historical Canadian approach which divides Quebec identity along ethnic lines, French-Canadian and English-Canadian, and substitute a civic approach which bases the identity of the people of Quebec on welcome and inclusion, thanks to a common language, French, and a common culture made up of all its component parts.'

French in public signage and commercial advertising appear to have been resolved, at least at the level of policy, following battles reaching the Supreme Court of Canada, though the data on imposition of penalties published by the OQLF indicate that, in practice, not all Quebecers subscribe to the letter of the law and monitoring is therefore necessary to ensure compliance. With regard to access to instruction in the minority language in Canada, whether French or English, the situation continues to be problematic, as parents assert their rights under the Canadian Charter or anglophone and allophone parents contest the restrictions placed on access to instruction in English in Quebec. The question of access of allophones to education in English remains a crucial one in Quebec, linked as it is to the fear of anglicisation of immigrants. The Quebec Charter has proved to be instrumental in halting this process of anglicisation of young immigrants, the majority of whom were in the English school system before its enactment. This measure alone has played a central role in assuring the future of French in the province.

Despite the increased self-confidence of *Québécois* and the encouraging signs of vibrancy of French in the province, many feel that there is no room for complacency and that vigilance should remain the order of the day. The President of the *Commission des États généraux sur la situation et l'avenir de la langue française au Québec*, Gérald Larose, points out that 'les acquis sont fragiles' ('gains are fragile') (Larose, 2001: 1), in the face of globalisation and new information and communication technologies. Another commentator reflects on the achievements of the Quebec Charter as an instrument of language policy in the following terms, suggesting that the dilemmas are ones which may never be resolved, given that they are grounded in issues of identity, which, of necessity, are susceptible to change emanating from both internal and external sources:

> D'une certaine manière, la Charte de la langue française a atténué la crise linguistique qui a occupé la scène politique québécoise des années 1960–1970. Mais les assauts répétés que la Charte a subis et subit toujours devant les tribunaux et dans certains médias montrent que cette crise n'est pas totalement résolue, et ne le sera peut-être pas dans un avenir prévisible. La crise linguistique demeure latente, parce que les grands dilemmes des années 1960–1970 peuvent toujours resurgir à l'occasion de l'évolution du contexte à la fois

canadien, nord-américain et mondial. Et cela, parce que ce sont des dilemmes identitaires, et que l'identité d'une collectivité est toujours en voie de se redéfinir par divers acteurs et intervenants de cette collectivité même. (Rocher, 2002: 24)[38]

Key Dates: Quebec

1910	Loi Lavergne
1961	Establishment of the *Ministère des Affaires culturelles* and the *Office de la langue française*
1967	French obligatory on the labelling of agricultural products
1968	Gendron Commission
1969	Bill 63 *Loi pour promouvoir la langue française au Québec*
1970	French required for non-Canadians applying to practise a profession

---

38 'To some extent, the Charter of the French language has attenuated the linguistic crisis which occupied the Quebec political scene in the 1960s and 1970s. But the repeated attacks which the Charter has suffered and continues to suffer before the courts and in some media show that this crisis is not completely resolved, and may not be resolved in the foreseeable future. The linguistic crisis remains latent, because the great dilemmas of the 1960s and 1970s could resurface in the event of a change in the Canadian, North American or global context. The reason is that they are dilemmas of identity, and because the identity of a collectivity is always being redefined by members of that collectivity itself.'

1974	Bill 22 *Loi sur la langue officielle*
1977	Bill 101 *Charte de la langue française*
1984	Supreme Court judgment on language of instruction (Quebec Protestant School Boards)
1988	Supreme Court judgment on external signage
1988	Bill 178 (derogation on external signage)
1993	Bill 86

4   The changing linguistic landscape of Canada

Introduction

The linguistic landscape of Canada has changed beyond recognition over the centuries since the arrival of the French in the sixteenth and seventeenth centuries. The census of population, carried out every five years, is a major source of data on the demographic linguistic situation and on developing trends. In terms of data on language, the census gives very valuable information on the relative weight of different language groups, allowing for detailed analysis of a variety of language issues including the identification of trends over time at national and provincial levels. The first census of the twenty-first century, taken in 2001, provides an abundance of material for an analysis of the linguistic composition of Canada, a country with a population of around 30 million people, at the beginning of the new millennium. This chapter focuses on data collected by the census, and the results and conclusions which may be drawn, firstly for Canada and Canada less Quebec, and secondly, for the province of Quebec.

Census data in Canada

By contrast with many other countries (even those which also boast more than one official language)[1] Canada collects a wealth of census data on language, which is then made available for analysis by Statistics Canada. In addition, Statistics Canada publishes a Census Dictionary which supplies background information on the definitions, concepts and variables used in the preparation and compilation of census data (Canada. Statistics Canada, 2004).[2] From a methodological point of view, it is useful to note that not all households receive the same questionnaire. Four out of five households receive a short form which contains seven questions, including one on Mother Tongue. One in five households receives the long form, which contains an additional fifty-two questions, including three further questions on language. According to Statistics Canada, this sampling method yields 'high-quality data while reducing costs and response burden'.[3]

The most recent census for which data are available was taken on 15 May 2001 and most of the language data from it were released on 10 December 2002.[4] Language data were collected for the first time in four rather than in three categories, as had been the case prior to 2001:

1   The census questionnaire for Ireland (2006), a country with two official languages, Irish and English, has only one question on language, with two parts: Q.12, 'Can you speak Irish?; Answer 'yes' or 'no'; If yes, do you speak Irish (1) daily within the educational system, (2) daily outside the educational system, (3) weekly, (4) less often, (4) never.' (See Conrick (2006) for further comparative discussion).

2   As well as providing information on the current situation, the Census Dictionary also gives information from a historical perspective in the Appendices; for example, Appendix A deals with 'Census Questionnaire Content and Derived Variables Since Confederation'.

3   See the website of Statistics Canada for further information on data collection in the census. Data on the content of the 2001 questionnaires are available at www.statcan.ca/english/census96/2001/population/content.htm.

4   Another census of population was taken on 16 May 2006, with release dates for the main language questions on 14 November 2007 and 12 February 2008 for language at work.

- Mother Tongue
- Home Language
- Knowledge of Official Languages
- Language at Work

Mother Tongue,[5] the only language question asked of the entire population, is defined for the purposes of the 2001 Census as 'the first language learned at home in childhood and still understood by the individual at the time of the census' (Canada. Statistics Canada, 2004). A question on Mother Tongue was first asked in a census in 1901, and this question has figured in all censuses since 1971, giving a rich source of data for the thirty-year period, during which much attention was devoted to language policy issues at both federal and provincial levels.

The question on Home Language was first asked in 1971, of a one-fifth sample. In Census 2001 it is defined as 'the language spoken most often or on a regular basis at home by the individual at the time of the census' (Canada. Statistics Canada, 2004). Until the census of 1996, this question had only one part, concerning the language spoken most often at home. Census 2001 added a part (b), seeking information on any other languages spoken on a regular basis at home, but not as frequently as the language reported in part (a) of the question.

Information on Knowledge of Official Languages was sought first in 1901, and it has been sought on all censuses but one[6] since 1971. The question refers to the ability to 'carry on a conversation of some length on various topics' in English or French (Canada. Statistics Canada, 2004). The possible responses were: English only; French only; both English and French; neither English nor French. It should be borne in mind that, as this information is self-reported, it is necessarily a subjective rather than an objective measure of language competence.

---

5   Linguists would normally use the term 'first language', or L1, rather than Mother Tongue. The term Mother Tongue is retained here for clarity and consistency, as it is the term commonly used in the context of the census.

6   Questions on Home Language and Knowledge of Official Languages were not asked in the 1976 census.

In addition to the three questions mentioned previously, Census 2001 collected for the first time further information on language in the new category of language spoken at work. These data were released on 11 February 2003. The question on language of work was a two-part one, seeking information on 'the language used most often at work by the individual at the time of the census' and on any 'other languages used at work on a regular basis' (Canada. Statistics Canada, 2004). Data from this category provide very valuable information on language use in the public domain, thus complementing the information from the categories of Mother Tongue and Home Language which are obviously focussed on the private domain. Over time, when data become available from further censuses, it will be possible to build up a more comprehensive picture, on an ongoing basis, of language use in both the private and public domains.

As well as being of concern to a wide range of interested parties including researchers on language, conclusions drawn from these data have an obvious impact on decision making in many areas of economic and social policy, including the areas of language policy and planning. The intrinsic connection between the census data and the formulation and implementation of policy is made explicit by Statistics Canada in its comments on the content of the 2001 census questionnaires:

> These data will be used to protect the rights of Canadians under the Canadian Charter of Rights and Freedoms. They will also be used in forecasting language-training requirements and in determining where services must be provided to comply with the Official Languages Act. (www.statcan.ca/ english/census96/2001/population/content.htm)

Results of Census 2001: Canada

Canada: Mother Tongue

The results of Census 2001 show that Mother Tongue speakers of the two official languages together account for 82% of the Canadian population of close to 30 million, with a clear majority of English speakers (59.1%), and French as the second most important language (22.9%). Despite the continued preponderance of the two official language groups, Canada has become much more multilingual, as is evidenced by the fact that more than a hundred languages in total were reported as Mother Tongue, and allophones (speakers of a language other than English or French) are the only group which shows an increase in percentage share of the population since the previous census of 1996. One of the difficulties posed by the categorisation of speakers of all languages other than English and French into one group, allophones, is that it is a very heterogeneous group, which includes both First Nations and immigrants. Apart from English and French, the most common first languages are Chinese,[7] Italian, German, Punjabi and Spanish, with the order of the first three non-official languages remaining unchanged since the previous census.[8]

---

7   The percentage of Chinese Mother Tongue speakers is 2.9%, almost 872,000 people, increased from 2.6% in 1996.

8   The most frequent First Nations languages as Mother Tongue were Cree (80,000), Inuktitut (29,700) and Ojibway (23,500) (Canada. Statistics Canada, 2002: 6).

Year	Anglophones	Francophones	Allophones
1971	60.1%	26.9%	13.0%
1991	60.4%	24.3%	15.3%
1996	59.8%	23.5%	16.6%
2001	59.1%	22.9%	18.0%

Table 4.1: Canada by Mother Tongue, share of population, 1971, 1991,
1996, and 2001[9]
Source: Statistics Canada, Census of population

It is clear from Table 4.1 that the overall *share* of the population of both official language groups has continued to decline over the last three censuses, with francophones showing a decline consistently over the thirty-year period since 1971. This is the case despite the fact that the *numbers* of both groups have grown since 1991 (see Table 4.2). There has been a corresponding increase in the overall share of allophones, which has been sustained at each census during the same period. Allophones recorded an increase in numbers as well as share of the population, a trend which is accounted for by the level of immigration to Canada during the period. Table 4.2 shows the increase in numbers for the three groups between 1991 and 2001.

Year	Anglophones	Francophones	Allophones
1991	16,311,210	6,562,060	4,120,770
2001	17,521,880	6,782,320	5,334,770

Table 4.2: Canada by Mother Tongue, numbers, 1991 and 2001
Source: Statistics Canada, Census of population

9   Statistical information used in this chapter has been sourced from Statistics Canada, in particular, Statistics Canada (2002) and Statistics Canada (2003). The tables have been compiled by the author. A methodological note in *Profile of languages in Canada: English, French and many others*, (Canada. Statistics Canada, 2002: 25) explains how single and multiple responses were handled, multiple responses being when respondents reported having, for example, two Mother Tongues. Generally, multiple responses were divided equally between the languages, but when an analysis was done of a specific language group, all responses, single and multiple, were counted in order to arrive at the relative share of the group.

Though the total number of francophones in Canada increased to almost 6.8 million in 2001, the growth rate has slowed down considerably since the previous census period. This is explained by Statistics Canada as follows:

> The census enumerated almost 6.8 million francophones, a 1.1% increase from 1996, just half the growth rate of 2.3% from 1991 to 1996. This slowdown is attributed to a decline in the number of francophone children aged four and under. In addition, the francophone population is aging. The proportion of seniors aged 65 and over increased from 11.2% in 1996 to 12.5% in 2001.

These statistics confirm why those interested in the fate of French are concerned about the demographic trends which show that the francophone population is shrinking in relative terms. The demographic pattern of more speakers in the older category is a negative indicator for the future of the language group. It is obvious, as a consequence of this situation, why language transfer patterns of immigrants are of such interest to language planners in Quebec who are concerned about the maintenance of the position and status of French in the province. In the context of a slowdown in growth of the younger francophone population, the encouragement of immigrants to transfer to French rather than English is a key element of provincial policy in Quebec with regard to providing for and protecting the future of the French language. The policy of restricting access to education in English in Quebec (discussed in Chapter 3), which has a significant impact on immigrants, needs to be contextualised in relation to the demographic patterns which are evident from trends in census data identified over the past thirty years.

With regard to the position of French as Mother Tongue at provincial level, the situation is that Quebec continues to be the only province in which francophones are in the majority, with 81.4% share of the population. The position of the French language in provinces outside Quebec is of particular interest, given its status as an official minority language everywhere except Quebec. The tendency towards greater concentration of francophones in Quebec has been maintained in 2001, with percentages for Canada less Quebec declining from 4.8% to 4.4% between 1991and 2001, though the numbers have increased during the period, from 976,415 to 980,270 (Canada.

Statistics Canada, 2002: 26). The data may be interpreted in more than one way, depending on whether greater weight is attributed to numbers or the relative percentage share of the population. Churchill (1998: 12) interprets the situation somewhat positively, as her analysis of trends over the previous three decades is based on the growth in numbers:

> The French-speaking communities in Canada outside Quebec continue to grow and to receive small numbers of French-speaking immigrants from abroad. The growth is, however, slower than that of the non-French population.

However the data are interpreted, it remains the case that the vast majority of francophones are located in the three eastern provinces of Quebec, New Brunswick and Ontario, and that francophone minorities outside Quebec are subject to the increasing influence of assimilation towards English, for various reasons including their geographical situation, marriage patterns and anglophone immigration. Percentages of francophones in the provinces and territories are detailed in Table 4.3 (along with information in the category of Home Language).

Province/Territory	Mother Tongue %	Home Language %
Newfoundland and Labrador	0.5	0.2
Prince Edward Island	4.4	2.1
Nova Scotia	3.9	2.2
New Brunswick	33.2	30.3
Ontario	4.5	2.7
Quebec	81.4	83.1
Manitoba	4.2	1.9
Saskatchewan	1.9	0.5
Alberta	2.1	0.7
British Columbia	1.5	0.4
Yukon Territory	3.3	1.5
Northwest Territories	2.7	1.1
Nunavut	1.5	0.8
Canada less Quebec	4.4	2.7

Table 4.3: French in Canada, Mother Tongue and Home Language,
provinces and territories and Canada less Quebec, 2001
Source: Statistics Canada, Census of population

The statistics show clearly that the share of the francophone population overall outside Quebec is relatively small and has decreased further since 1991. The only province or territory where francophones are numbered in double figure percentages is New Brunswick, with 33.2% (down from 34% in 1991). Elsewhere, Newfoundland and Labrador recorded the lowest percentage, with only 0.5% (the same percentage as in 1991). When growth rate figures are examined, they show that the biggest decrease for the period 1996–2001 was recorded in Manitoba, at 6.5%, an acceleration of the decrease of 3.3% during the previous census period (1991–1996). Two provinces, Alberta and Ontario, reversed a decline recorded in the 1991–1996 period and show growth rates of 12.6% and 1.9%, respectively, for 1996–2001.

While using the data collected on Mother Tongue has clear advantages from the point of view of the availability of comparative historical data, the picture of the linguistic landscape of Canada which is the result is not necessarily as useful as it was some decades ago. The historical connection between language and cultural origin is no longer what it was at the time (the 1960s) when the Royal Commission on Bilingualism and Biculturalism carried out its work. As present-day Canada is composed of a multiplicity of ethnicities and diverse language groups, other linguistic data, such as first official language learned, are increasingly useful in terms of determining membership of an official language community.[10] It is becoming increasingly anachronistic to use the term 'francophone' primarily to designate people of French ethnic origin, given the numbers of French speakers who are not of French ethnic origin. It may be ultimately more useful in terms of gathering linguistic data to define 'francophone', in purely linguistic (rather than cultural or historical) terms as 'French-speaking'.

10   See Churchill (1998: 8–10) for further discussion of this issue.

Canada: Home Language

The statistics in the category of Home Language are, in many ways, more significant from a linguistic point of view than those for Mother Tongue, since they show any patterns of transfer from the Mother Tongue to another language. The language of the home is the one most likely to be passed on to children, whatever the linguistic or ethnic background of the parents. Table 4.4 details the numbers and share of the population in the Home Language category for the period 1991–2001.

Year	English		French		Non-official language	
	Numbers	Percentages	Numbers	Percentages	Numbers	Percentages
1991	18,440,535	68.3%	6,288,425	23.3%	2,265,075	8.4%
2001	20,011,535	67.5%	6,531,375	22.0%	3,096,110	10.5%

Table 4.4: Canada by Home Language, 1991 and 2001
Source: Statistics Canada, Census of population

A comparison with the statistics for Mother Tongue shows some similar trends since 1991: increases in the numbers of those speaking English and French, and decreases in the corresponding percentages, i.e., in share of the population, while both the numbers and percentages of those speaking non-official languages have increased.

Nine out of ten people in Canada speak English or French most often at home (Canada. Statistics Canada, 2002: 6). Non-official languages are spoken at home less frequently (10.5%) than they are reported as Mother Tongue (18%), (see Tables 4.1 and 4.2 above), indicating a language shift on the part of allophones to the official languages. In the case of English, the share of the population speaking English at home is considerably higher (67.5%) than the proportion who reported the language as their Mother Tongue (59.1%), underlining the strong appeal of transfer to English. This contrasts with the situation of French, which shows a lower percentage for Home Language (22.0%) than for Mother Tongue (22.9%). This is a very discouraging statistic in terms of the prospects of the francophone population, for whom the fear of assimilation continues to be omnipresent.[11]

When the breakdown for provinces and territories is analysed, it is clear that fewer francophones outside Quebec speak French most often at home. Statistics Canada describes and explains the situation in the following way:

> Between 1996 and 2001, the proportion of francophones who spoke a language other than French most often at home increased again in every province and territory and territory except the Northwest Territories [...] The growth in language transfers among francophones outside Quebec was due partly to the increase in the proportion of francophones who formed conjugal unions with anglophones. In many of these couples, the spouse whose mother tongue is French speaks English most often at home. (Canada, Statistics Canada, 2002: 11–12)

This statistical information highlights the continuing decline of French as Home Language outside Quebec, in particular the level of assimilation towards English. This may not be surprising, given the low percentage of French as Mother Tongue in all provinces outside Quebec except New Brunswick (discussed above). It points to the need for official language programmes, such as those promoted by the Office of the Commissioner of Official Languages, supporting the minority official language communities, if the decline is to be slowed down or halted.

Statistics Canada attempts to strike a positive note by pointing out that, though transfers to English have increased since 1996, francophones have not necessarily abandoned their Mother Tongue entirely, still speaking it regularly at home.[12] In New Brunswick, for example, 10.5% of francophones use English most often at home, an increase on the figure of 9.7% in 1996, but almost half of them

11 See Castonguay (1994) for discussion of assimilation, between 1971 and 1986. The text also reviews studies of the status of French which were contemporaneous to the B&B and Gendron Commissions, all of which report concern about the precariousness of the situation of French.
12 Changes to the 2001 Census question on Home Language mean that more detailed information is available in this regard than was the case in previous censuses.

(48.4%) still continue to use French regularly. The transfer rate is even higher in other provinces, such as Ontario, where 40.3% of francophones reported using English most often at home, though 42.7% of these still use French on a regular basis at home (Canada, Statistics Canada, 2002: 11). The percentage of transfers is even higher for Manitoba, with 54.7% of francophones using English most often at home and fewer of these (37.4%) still speaking French regularly. Despite the professed optimism of the Statistics Canada report, the fact remains that there is a marked trend towards francophones transferring to English as the principal language of the home. The fact that many maintain regular use of French simply points to increased levels of bilingualism among francophones, though, as the statistics for Knowledge of Official Languages show, this is not matched by anything approaching the same level of proficiency in French among the anglophone population.

Canada: Knowledge of Official Languages

Statistics in this category provide information on levels of bilingualism in English and French. They also give information on multilingualism, in the case of allophones who already speak a language or languages other than French or English. Percentages for Knowledge of Official Languages in 2001 for the provinces and territories and for Canada less Quebec are listed in Table 4.5.

There has been an increase in the rate of bilingualism in Canada overall and in all provinces and territories except Manitoba and Saskatchewan. This is very encouraging news for policy makers promoting bilingualism. The percentage of bilinguals in the population was recorded as 17.7%, up from 17% in 1996, with 5,231,500 Canadians declaring themselves to be bilingual, as opposed to 4,841,300 in 1996, an increase of 8.1%. However, despite the overall increase in rates of bilingualism, there are very noticeable differences between provinces when the percentages are broken down.

	1991	1996	2001
Canada	16.3	17.0	17.7
Newfoundland and Labrador	3.3	3.9	4.1
Prince Edward Island	10.1	11.0	12.0
Nova Scotia	8.6	9.3	10.1
New Brunswick	29.5	32.6	34.2
Quebec	35.4	37.8	40.8
Ontario	11.4	11.6	11.7
Manitoba	9.2	9.4	9.3
Saskatchewan	5.2	5.2	5.1
Alberta	6.6	6.7	6.9
British Columbia	6.4	6.7	7.0
Yukon Territory	9.3	10.5	10.1
Northwest Territories		7.7	8.3
Nunavut		4.1	3.8
Canada less Quebec	9.8	10.2	10.3

Table 4.5: Canada by Knowledge of Official Languages, provinces and territories
and Canada less Quebec, percentages, 1991, 1996 and 2001
Source: Statistics Canada, Census of population

The most obvious comment that can be made on the statistics listed in Table 4.5 is that Quebec is the most bilingual province, and New Brunswick is in second place, with the rate for these provinces significantly above the figure for the country as a whole and figures for other provinces and territories. By contrast, the figure for Canada less Quebec is much lower at 10.3%. Consequently, one might say that the high rate of bilingualism in Quebec contributes significantly to current levels of bilingualism in Canada. Given that Quebec is predominantly francophone, the only conclusion that can be reached is that francophones are far more likely to be bilingual, i.e., they are more likely to be able to speak English than anglophones are to speak French. This is indeed what is confirmed when the breakdown of percentages according to language group is examined.

The figures analysed by language group (Table 4.6), reveal some startling results. Most notably, 43.4% of francophones in Canada reported themselves as being bilingual, while only 9.0% of anglophones did so. This information paints a very different picture of the distribution of bilingualism from that suggested by the 17.7%

undifferentiated figure for the whole country, pointing out the wide variation which exists between the competence in French of anglophones as opposed to the much higher levels of competence in English of francophones. Clearly, bilingualism features as a characteristic of the linguistic behaviour of many more francophones than anglophones.

Date	Anglophone	Francophone	Allophone
1991	8.2%	38.6%	11.3%
1996	8.8%	40.8%	11.2%
2001	9.0%	43.4%	11.8%

Table 4.6: Canada by Knowledge of Official Languages,
1991, 1996 and 2001
Source: Statistics Canada, Census of population

A further point of note is that bilingualism is 'losing some ground among young anglophones outside Quebec' (Canada. Statistics Canada, 2002: 13). This is evident when the statistics are broken down according to age group. Normally for anglophones outside Quebec, the rate of bilingualism is at its peak in the 15–19 age group, due to acquisition of French as a second language at school or in immersion programmes. The rate of bilingualism for this group was 16.3% in 1996, but it declined to 14.7% in 2001. This pattern characterised all provinces west of Quebec; only Newfoundland and Labrador and Nova Scotia showed an increase. As this group of anglophones gets older, they tend to become less bilingual. The group which was aged 15–19 in 1996 was five years older (20–24) in 2001, and the figure for bilingualism had dropped from 16.3% to 13.5%, replicating the pattern from 1991–1996. It appears that bilingualism for young anglophones outside Quebec is a phenomenon which involves primarily the high school years.

As information in this category was sought for the first time in 2001, it is obviously not possible to make comparisons with other census periods. However, the data collected give a detailed picture, a snapshot of the current state of play with regard to language use in the public domain of the workplace. For the purposes of the census, workers were defined as: 'People aged 15 years and over who worked between January 1, 2000 and May 15, 2001' (Canada. Statistics Canada, 2003: 11).

The results show that almost 15% of Canadian workers, about 2.5 million people, use more than one language at work. When the results are broken down by language group, significant disparities are evident, with both francophones and allophones far ahead of anglophones in the context of bilingualism or multilingualism at work. The figures by language group for Canada less Quebec again show the high rate of use of another language by francophones outside Quebec. The national rate for anglophones is very low at 4.3%, and even lower for Canada less Quebec at 2.6%, (see Table 4.7).

	All workers	Francophones	Anglophones	Allophones
Canada	14.6%	32.9%	4.3%	25.6%
Canada less Quebec	8.4%	53.3%	2.6%	20.0%

Table 4.7: Proportion of workers using more than one language at work,
by language group, Canada and Canada less Quebec, 2001
Source: Statistics Canada, Census of population

Statistics Canada (Canada. Statistics Canada, 2003: 5) points out, not surprisingly, that:

> The use of more than one language at work is closely related to the knowledge of languages among these groups. In Canada, 54% of francophone workers are English-French bilingual, compared with 10% of anglophones and 14% of allophones.

The figures may be broken down further, to provide information on use of specific languages. Tables 4.8 and 4.9 give details of use of

French and English at work, by reference to the three language group categories. (The figures for the categories 'most often' and 'regularly' are combined in the presentation of these data.)

	Francophones	Anglophones	Allophones
Canada	94.3%	4.0%	11.4%
Canada less Quebec	67.4%	2.1%	1.8%

Table 4.8: Use of French at work, by language group,
Canada and Canada less Quebec, 2001
Source: Statistics Canada, Census of population

	Francophones	Anglophones	Allophones
Canada	38.5%	99.7%	92.5%
Canada less Quebec	85.6%	99.9%	95.4%

Table 4.9: Use of English at work, by language group,
Canada and Canada less Quebec, 2001
Source: Statistics Canada, Census of population

The figures in Tables 4.8 and 4.9 show clearly the dominance of English as the language used most often or regularly in the workplace by anglophones and allophones. The percentage of francophones who use English (38.5%) is way above the figure for anglophones who use French (4.0%). These figures confirm the greater propensity of francophones to use another language, notably English, at work.

With regard to use of French at work in Canada less Quebec, 67.4% of the 566,000 francophone workers outside Quebec use French most often or regularly. The province with the highest rate is New Brunswick, with 92%. This tallies with the status of New Brunswick as the only officially bilingual province, and with statistics in the other related census categories. The figure for Ontario's 289,000 francophone workers is significantly lower at 69%.

The information on language use at work means that a more complete linguistic picture of Canada is now available. In the case of anglophones, the figures for use of French show similar results to those in the category of Knowledge of Official Languages. In the case of francophones, the results show that there is a correlation between the use of French in the home and in the workplace. In addition,

French is obviously present in the workplace and therefore not confined to being a language of the home.

Results of Census 2001: Quebec

Language data from the census for Quebec differ significantly from those of other provinces, given the unique position of Quebec as the only province in which francophones are in the majority. Quebec is linguistically, as well as historically and culturally, a province apart from the rest of Canada. This is reflected in the presentation of census data by Statistics Canada, as figures are usually provided for each province and territory, with the addition of a global figure for Canada less Quebec.

Quebec: Mother Tongue

Table 4.10 shows the breakdown by Mother Tongue, numbers and share of the population for the province of Quebec since 1991.

Date	Francophones		Anglophones		Allophones	
	Numbers	Percentages	Numbers	Percentages	Numbers	Percentages
1991	5,585,650	82.0	626,200	9.2	598,450	8.8
1996	5,741,430	81.5	621,860	8.8	681,785	9.7
2001	5,802,020	81.4	591,365	8.3	732,160	10.3

Table 4.10: Quebec by Mother Tongue, 1991, 1996 and 2001
Source: Statistics Canada, Census of population

Both francophones and allophones recorded an increase in numbers over the census periods between 1991 and 2001, though only allophones recorded a corresponding increase in percentage share of the population. The most common Mother Tongues other than English or French were Italian, Arabic and Spanish. Statistics Canada comments on the position of francophones in Quebec in the following terms:

In Quebec, the francophone population increased by about 60,600 from 1996 to 2001, less than half the gain during the previous five-year period. This slowdown was the result of a net loss through interprovincial migration, and a decline in the number of francophone children aged four and under. (Canada. Statistics Canada, 2002: 9)

In the case of anglophones, the trend has been towards a decline, which accelerated between 1996 and 2001, with numbers dropping by 30,495, compared with a drop of 4,340 in the previous census period. The decrease was largely due to migration of anglophones to other provinces, notably Ontario, and to the decline in children under four, similar to that noted for francophones. The phenomenon of anglophones migrating from Quebec has been linked for some time to a level of dissatisfaction with the language policies pursued by the provincial government. The current situation is that anglophones in Quebec are now outnumbered collectively by allophones, a situation first recorded by the 1996 census.

The linguistic picture of the Montreal Urban Community (MUC) (*Communauté urbaine de Montréal*) is always of major interest, because of its size and position as one of the three biggest urban centres in Canada (along with Toronto and Vancouver).[13] One of the results of the 2001 census which caused a stir was the fact that the number of francophones in Montreal increased for the first time since 1971, growing by 14,500, due particularly to the arrival of international French-speaking immigrants, but also to the arrival of francophones from other provinces and from other regions of Quebec.[14] It

13   The census metropolitan area of Montreal, with a population of just over 3.7 million, accounts for 52% of the population of Quebec and 12% of the population of Canada.

14   About 3,000 Francophones left Quebec between 1996 and 2001, a large reduction from the 50,400 departures recorded between 1991 and 1996. These were compensated for by the increase in incoming numbers, leading to a net gain of 14,500. For journalistic commentary on these figures, see for example: Sylvain Larocque, 'Une première en 30 ans: Le nombre de francophones a crû à Montréal', *Presse canadienne*, 10 December 2002 (available at www.cyberpresse.ca) and Valérie Dufour, 'Recensement 2001 – Plus de Montréalais francophones, mais…le poids démographique des francophones diminue', *Le Devoir*, 11 December 2002.

had been predicted that the francophone population of Montreal would decrease significantly. In a study carried out on demographic trends, Marc Termote (1994: 259) had forecast a decline in the francophone population in Quebec, and in particular in Montreal:

> La décroissance démographique du Québec semble inéluctable [...] Cette décroissance sera accompagnée d'une réduction de la part du groupe francophone au sein de la population québécoise (et de la population québécoise au sein de l'ensemble canadien), selon un clivage qui verrait le pourcentage de francophones dans la région de Montréal (et surtout sur l'île de Montréal) baisser considérablement [...] Tant que les francophones maintiendront un régime de sous-fécondité par rapport aux non-francophones, et tant que l'immigration internationale sera élevée, la part des francophones diminuera inéluctablement.[15]

Contrary to Termote's prediction, the role of international immigration has become a positive factor for the growth of francophone numbers. This increase inevitably had an effect also on the proportion of those with French as Home Language in Montreal.

Quebec: Home Language

The numbers recorded with French as the language spoken most often at home increased by 266,600 in Quebec over the ten-year period since the 1991 census. However, in contrast to the Mother Tongue category, the corresponding percentage of the population also increased, though it is a very small one, i.e., 0.1%. Table 4.11 details the situation with regard to Home Language in Quebec from the 1991 to the 2001 census.

---

15 'The demographic decline of Quebec seems unavoidable. [...] This decline will be accompanied by a reduction in the francophone share of the population of Quebec (and of the Quebec population of Canada as a whole) according to a regional division which would show a considerable lowering of the percentage of francophones in the metropolitan region of Montreal (and especially on the island of Montreal). [...] As long as francophones maintain a low fertility rate compared with non-francophones, and as long as international immigration is high, the share of francophones will decrease unavoidably.'

	French		English		Non-official language	
Date	Numbers	Percentages	Numbers	Percentages	Numbers	Percentages
1991	5,651,790	83.0	761,810	11.2	396,695	5.8
1996	5,830,080	82.8	762,455	10.8	452,540	6.4
2001	5,918,390	83.1	746,895	10.5	460,295	6.5

Table 4.11: Quebec by Home Language, 1991, 1996 and 2001
Source: Statistics Canada, Census of population

When the proportion of allophones speaking French most often at home in Quebec is analysed, it emerges that the percentage has increased significantly since the 1991 census, while the proportion of allophones speaking English most often decreased over the same period (see Table 4.12).

	French	English
1991	15.4%	24.1%
1996	16.6%	22.4%
2001	20.4%	22.1%

Table 4.12: Quebec, proportion of allophones speaking French
or English most often at home, 1991, 1996 and 2001
Source: Statistics Canada, Census of population

These figures indicate an acceleration in the transfer rate to French among allophones, with about 46% of those who did transfer to English or French transferring to French, as opposed to 39% in 1996. The figure for transfer to English was 54%, a drop from 61% in 1996 (Canada. Statistics Canada, 2002: 12). The changes in transfer rates point to the success of the language policies implemented in Quebec, designed to achieve this end. Furthermore, immigrants in the two youngest categories, 0–14 and 15–19 show the highest rates of transfer to French, (55% and 56.8%, respectively).

> ... c'est manifestement parmi les allophones les plus jeunes que les transferts linguistiques sont proportionnellement plus favorables au français [...] Par contre, pour les groupes plus âgés, l'anglais est plus utilisé que le français sur le plan des transferts linguistiques. (Amireault, 2004: 59)[16]

16 'It is manifestly among the youngest allophones that language transfers are proportionately more favourable to French [...] Conversely, in the case of the

This trend is a very encouraging one for the future of French, suggesting that the current overall transfer figures, favouring transfer to English (54%) rather than French (46%), might be reversed in the not too distant future, given such demographic indicators.

The role of language policy alone cannot be said to account entirely for the increase in rates of transfer to French. Another argument is related to the country of origin of immigrants.[17] In the Montreal Urban Community, the biggest centre of population in Quebec, there was an increase, over the previous fifteen years, in allophones from groups with Arabic, Spanish and Creole as Mother Tongue. Immigrants from these linguistic backgrounds are more likely to transfer to French than to English.[18]

Following the release of the census data in 2002, the Montreal daily newspaper *La Presse* published an article entitled: 'Recensement national: Montréal devient plus français' (Berger, F., 11 December 2002). Berger's conclusion stems from the fact that the percentage with French as Home Language in Montreal went up since 1996, a reversal of the trend in the previous census period, combined with the fact that the percentage with English as Home Language declined during the two previous census periods (see Table 4.13).[19]

Date	French		English		Non-official language	
	Numbers	Percentages	Numbers	Percentages	Numbers	Percentages
1991	1,004,520	57.4	454,020	26.0	290,800	16.6
1996	972,880	55.6	448,060	25.6	328,580	18.8
2001	1,005,670	56.4	444,560	25.0	332,370	18.6

Table 4.13: Montreal Urban Community by Home Language, 1991, 1996 and 2001
Source: Statistics Canada, Census of population

older groups, language transfers to English are more common than transfers to French.'

17 For information on immigration policy, see the website of the Quebec Government department, Relations avec les citoyens et Immigration, at www.immigration-quebec.gouv.qc.ca.

18 See Monnier (1993) for discussion of the linguistic choices made by immigrants up to 1991.

19 In the same article, Marc Termote is quoted as expressing surprise at this development.

In addition, allophones in Montreal speak French more frequently than in the past. Among allophones who transferred to either French or English, 41% transferred to French in 2001, as opposed to 36% in 1996. All of these figures point to significant gains for French as Home Language in Montreal, as in Quebec generally.

Quebec: Knowledge of Official Languages

As noted in the section on Knowledge of Official Languages in Canada, there is a striking difference between rates of bilingualism for Quebec and those for the rest of Canada. Quebec is by far the most bilingual province, with a rate of 40.8%, by contrast with the rate for Canada less Quebec, at 10.3%. It may seem somewhat ironic that Quebec, the province which has on more than one occasion set itself apart from the Canadian mainstream by holding referenda on possible secession, is also the province which most closely reflects federal government policy in the area of bilingualism.

When the figures for Quebec are broken down by language group, they show interesting results, in particular, a very high rate of bilingualism for anglophones, very much in contrast to the national picture.

Date	Anglophone	Francophone	Allophone
1991	58.4%	31.3%	46.5%
1996	61.7%	33.7%	46.7%
2001	66.1%	36.6%	50.4%

Table 4.14: Quebec, rate of English-French bilingualism by language groups,
1991, 1996 and 2001
Source: Statistics Canada, Census of population

The rate for anglophones in Quebec, at 66.1%, is far in excess of the national figure of 9% for this language group. This situation distinguishes Quebec anglophones from those in the rest of Canada, in terms of their command of French. The rate for anglophones in Canada less Quebec is only 7.1%.

Given the growth of bilingualism among the anglophone and allophone groups, as evidenced by Table 4.14, it can be concluded that French, as a second or third language, is indeed progressing in Quebec. This again points to a measure of the success of the province's language policies. With regard to the francophone population, it is also true that bilingualism is progressing in that language group. Those interested in promoting the monolingual character of Quebec may not be quite so pleased with this statistic, as it means an increase in the ability of francophones to speak English. Federal policies on bilingualism are succeeding more in Quebec than elsewhere, making Quebec a 'model' province in this regard, and leading to greater multilingualism as well as bilingualism in the province.

Quebec: Language at Work

As in other categories, the figures for use of another language at work show a different picture for Quebec than for Canada as a whole. The figure for all workers is the second highest in Canada, at 35.2%, surpassed only by Nunavut, with 56.4%. New Brunswick has the third highest level, with 25.4%. When the figures are broken down by language group, it becomes evident that there is a very striking contrast between anglophones using another language at work in Quebec, at 59.1%, and the rest of Canada, with the next highest figure being 20.2% for Nunavut, and all other provinces having figures below 10%.

	All workers	Francophones	Anglophones	Allophones
Quebec	35.2%	29.3%	59.1%	63.0%

Table 4.15: Quebec, proportion of workers
using more than one language at work, 2001
Source: Statistics Canada, Census of population

When the figures for use of the two official languages are analysed, the situation for francophones is clear: almost all use French at work, 95.7% 'most often', plus 3.3% 'regularly'. When Table 4.16 is compared with Table 4.8, Quebec anglophones are shown to be far ahead of anglophones in the rest of Canada (as was also the case in the Knowledge of Official Languages category) in their use of French at work.

	Francophones	Anglophones	Allophones
French	99.0%	65.3%	75.7%
English	30.2%	93.1%	72.5%

Table 4.16: Quebec, Use of English or French at work, 2001
Source: Statistics Canada, Census of population

The figures also show that French is the predominant language of work for allophones, who make up about 70% of Quebec's immigrant workers. The prevalence of French is even more apparent when the 75.7% figure for all allophones is broken down further: 56.5% of allophones use French 'most often' and 19% use it 'regularly', while nearly 49.8% use English 'most often' and 22.7% use it 'regularly'.[20] French was also the most prevalent language for allophone immigrant workers in Quebec in 2001, with about 60% of immigrant workers using French 'most often', along with 16% using it 'regularly' (as compared to English 'most often', 48%, and 'regularly', 22%).[21]

The figures for the Montreal Urban Community are very encouraging in terms of use of French, with almost 90% of those working there using French at work. This breaks down to about 74% using French 'most often' and 15% using it 'regularly'. According to Statistics Canada, the position of French is enhanced by the influx of workers from the northern and southern suburbs of the city. 'French was used most often at work by 69% of workers who lived in the MUC, and by 74% of those who worked there.' (Canada. Statistics Canada, 2003: 8). Based on recent study of the position of French in Montreal, Paquette (2006) reports that:

20   The figures for French and English used 'most often' add up to more than 100%, as some allophone workers reported using both languages equally often.
21   14% of allophone immigrant workers reported using both languages equally often.

[...] le français domine comme langue de service dans la région de Montréal. En effet, 85% des personnes interrogées se sont fait aborder et servir plus souvent en français qu'en anglais dans les commerces qu'elles ont fréquentés au cours des six derniers mois.[22]

The overall picture for Montreal in terms of its position as a major commercial centre working through the medium of French is a positive one.

Conclusion

Census data for Canada show an increasingly multilingual country, with more than a hundred languages reported as Mother Tongue and an increase in the relative weight of allophones in the population, and the consequent fall in relative weight of both the francophone and anglophone groups. The growth in cultural diversity, largely due to patterns of immigration, means that the traditional description of Canada's cultural reality as a case of 'two solitudes', based on the cultural and linguistic input of the founding peoples, French and British, may need to be revisited.[23]

The strength of the position of English as the major language throughout Canada is self-evident and its dominance is emphasised by the unassailable position it enjoys in the wider context of the continent of North America. The same cannot be said for the position of French in the country as a whole, except in Quebec, where it continues to be, by a long way, the majority language, with a strong position in the private and public domains in the areas of Mother Tongue, Home Language and Language at work. Trends such as the increase in language transfers of allophones to French rather than English at

22   'French dominates as the language of service in the Montreal area. In fact 85% of people surveyed were approached and served more often in French than in English in shops they went to during the past six months.'
23   Hugh MacLennan's classic novel, *Two Solitudes*, dealing with the clash of the two cultures, was first published in 1945.

home, and the high percentages among all language groups for use of French at work, are strong positive indicators of the status of French as a viable language not only in the home, but in the workplace in Quebec. The dichotomy between Quebec and the rest of Canada is clear, with big differences showing up in language data in all categories. This is true even in the case of Quebec anglophones, who are far more bilingual than their counterparts in the rest of the country. A further cause for concern is the general decline in fertility in Canada, with a rate of 1.76, which is more marked in Quebec, with a rate of 1.60 (Henripin, 2005: 63).[24]

The increasing concentration of francophones in Quebec, as evidenced by the figures for Mother Tongue, inevitably has as its corollary the decrease in francophones outside Quebec. In Canada less Quebec, the proportion of francophones is dwindling, with percentages in single digits, and the rates of bilingualism among anglophones are very much lower than they are for Quebec, giving rise to fears of assimilation of the French-speaking population. In addition, the French phenomenon may be seen as based on an east-west division, with the majority of francophones concentrated in eastern provinces, Quebec, New Brunswick and Ontario. Many of the studies carried out in the context of the B&B Commission already pointed to the concentration of a linguistic group in a region being a protection against assimilation, the converse being the vulnerability of linguistic groups which are dispersed.

> En effet, toutes les études concordaient sur ce point: plus un groupe linguistique est nombreux et concentré dans une région, plus il se trouve à l'abri de pertes par voie d'assimilation. (Castonguay, 1994: 14) [25]

---

24   In this article, Henripin compares data on ten European countries with Canada and Quebec. The data, from 2002, show Ireland having the highest rate at 2.26, with the figure for Quebec being the lowest.

25   'In fact, all the studies were in agreement on this point: the more numerous a linguistic group and the more concentrated it is geographically, the more protected it is against loss through assimilation.'

Despite the bilingual policies of the federal government, and the support provided by the Office of the Commissioner of Official Languages, the French-speaking communities in the rest of Canada are not in a very secure position. On the face of it, there is increasing polarisation between a French-speaking Quebec and a predominantly anglophone rest of Canada, as is clear from census data for Canada less Quebec. The political redefinition of Quebec in the 1970s, and the consequent fragmentation of French Canadian identity, has succeeded in increasing the dispersal and the marginalisation of the minority French-speaking communities in the rest of Canada. Quebec's gain in terms of strengthening its own identity based on the French language may be the loss of the francophone community of the rest of Canada.

5　French in multilingual Canada: the immersion project

Introduction

Canada is officially a bilingual society with varying degrees of bi-lingualism, depending on the region of Canada, ranging from Quebec on the one hand with a high number of bilinguals, to some of the Western provinces, for example, where the degree of bilingualism is slight. Until recently the linguistic situation appeared relatively un-complicated, if fraught in certain domains. Francophone speakers generally learned English relatively easily. This is due, among other factors, certainly to the dominant position of English world-wide and in Canada: speakers were, effectively, surrounded by English and so received input[1] with little effort. Anglophone speakers, on the other hand, do not necessarily learn French with the same ease. At the very least, input in French is not as readily available to anglophone speakers. A special enterprise has been necessary to put in place the acquisition of French as a second language by anglophone speakers; this is the French immersion project, which has won world-wide acclaim.

1　'Input' is defined in the *Longman Dictionary of Applied Linguistics* (Richards et al., 1992: 182) as: 'language which a learner hears or receives and from which he or she can learn'.

Canada: a multilingual society[2]

A new element has been added to the issue of linguistic choice. Recently Canada has had a growing population of allophones who choose between English or French as their official language of choice. In the past ten years, two and a half million immigrants have arrived in Canada. Fifty per cent of people living in Toronto were born outside Canada. Four out of ten immigrants in Vancouver are from China. Canada is an increasingly multicultural and multilingual new-world country, where the needs of both indigenous and immigrant groups are to the forefront at policy-making levels. Language issues have never been more intensely debated in Canada and this in a country where such issues have long been at the centre of political, economic and social debate. These debates play out against a background of institutional bilingualism, where every citizen has the right to use the official language of their choice when dealing with the federal government.[3]

The number of speakers whose first language is not English or French continues to grow in Canada. It follows that multiple languages are in contact, in a linguistically shifting situation, leading to political, social and linguistic outcomes which strongly define the identity of Canada and of Canadian citizens. Besides the official languages (English and French) consideration is given at federal and provincial levels to the Indigenous languages (Inuktitut, Ojibway, Cree-Montagnais-Naskapi, and about fifty other languages, most of them spoken only in Canada) and also the approximately two hundred immigrant Heritage languages spoken daily by immigrant groups.

For many Canadian citizens, as we have seen in Chapter 4, the acquisition of English and French as second languages is an on-going process, but the choice of which official language of Canada to learn

---

2   Multilingualism is understood to mean the presence and use of two or more languages in a country.

3   For a nuanced debate on citizenship see Cardinal (2004) and on multi-culturalism see Houle (2004), both of whom note and analyse the confrontation between ethnic diversity and social cohesion which exists in Canada today.

is no longer automatic or unproblematic (as it previously was when the vast majority of immigrants were of European origin) and involves issues of identity. The choice, acquisition and use of language are closely linked with issues of citizenship and community membership, which shifts constantly throughout the life of the speaker. This necessarily entails a continual process of socialisation, where individuals learn to act, think and feel, as well as to speak as members of other cultures, very much in the way children learn to become members of their primary community or culture. Canada has as a stated policy to recognize and encourage the cultural diversity of the different communities which live in Canada. In an increasingly multicultural Canada, citizens no longer perceive the traditional opposition between French Canada and English Canada as centrally defining. Nevertheless, the long-standing bilingual situation in Canada is still very much a force in the individual and the collective consciousness. This is true in the context of integration seen as an adaptive process which affects not only minority groups but also the welcoming society, where some values are understood to be non-negotiable.

As with native French speakers, those allophones who wish to learn English are surrounded by input, regardless of their area of residence. But, allophones who wish to learn French but reside outside French-speaking areas, must, like native English speakers who wish to learn French, depend on immersion. In the enterprise of acquiring a second language (L2) in Canada (where this L2 is French), the immersion experience can be seen very much as the defining experience for a majority of anglophone Canadians and now continues to be so for Canadian citizens of a multiplicity of first languages (L1). As we have seen (in chapter 4) the position of French outside of Quebec is increasingly vulnerable. There is one area, however, where French everywhere in Canada is very strongly supported: that of immersion education.

Immersion education in Canada

Language learning through immersion education has become a world-wide phenomenon since its beginnings in the 1960s. So widely known is it that it has influenced policy making and programmatic decisions in many domains including education and language teaching. It has contributed to improved relations between the anglophone and francophone communities. It has also contributed in an important way to theory of second language acquisition, earning accolades from numerous language experts, second language acquisition scholars, pedagogy experts and sociologists of language.

> Canadian immersion is not simply another successful language teaching programme – it may be the most successful programme ever recorded in the professional language-teaching literature. No programme has been as thoroughly studied and documented, and no programme, to my knowledge, has done as well. (Krashen, 1984: 61)

Immersion is a bilingual education where students receive part of their 'regular' education through an L2 and part through their L1. Many areas of research in second language acquisition have been influenced by the literature on immersion education including formal vs. informal contexts of language acquisition, age as a factor in L2 acquisition, negotiated meaning in native/non-native pairs, motivation for language learning, language acquisition through content learning and others.

Immersion education began in Canada in 1965 in St Lambert, a suburb of Montreal, where the first programme was established.[4] This programme was set up in response to pressure from anglophone parents who wanted their children to learn French from kindergarten level on. After the Quiet Revolution, Quebec's Bill 101 of 1977 declared French the only official language of Quebec and provided for linguistic rights of the majority French speaking citizens. Now, new non-English speaking Canadian citizens in Quebec are required to

---

4   In 1961, the Toronto French School had been established where young children already followed classes in French.

attend French medium schools, public signs are required to be in French and businesses are required to have the ability to conduct business in French (see Chapter 3). Parents in the sixties began to be aware of the necessity for their children to speak French for career success in the province of Quebec. In addition, they saw that proficiency in French was necessary for better relations between anglophone and francophone communities and that it would address the linguistic barriers between the English and French speaking communities. For these reasons, a group of parents were responsible principally for the start of immersion education. Much of the initial impetus found a focus in a meeting of Canadian Parents for French (CPF) with the first Commissioner of Official Languages, Keith Spicer (and his successors). It was felt that methods of language teaching at the time were inadequate both in terms of amount of time devoted to French and to traditional grammar and drill methods.

The success of the immersion venture was so great that other programmes were set up, first in Montreal, then throughout Canada and have since spread throughout the world. There are various contexts in which immersion education can take place. Canadian immersion, for instance, is a case of immersion for speakers of the majority language in the country (English) in a minority language (French). The student develops competence in a second language while keeping and developing their first language. This is known as additive bilingualism. Finland, where Finnish and Swedish are the two official languages, has immersion programs in Swedish. The first Swedish immersion program was established in 1987 and has been followed by others. The first programs were early total immersion, which is where young children learn everything through the L2. As in Canada, parents were aware of the economic and career advantages of the second language (Swedish in this case) for their children. An interesting aspect of the Finnish case is that, unlike the early immersion programs in Canada, Finnish immersion children were kept in contact with L1 Swedish children. As we will see later in relation to the Canadian case, the Finnish children having more contact with native speakers, their experience of the L2 was not restricted to classroom speech.[5] In Australia, there are immersion programmes in foreign languages – French and Chinese – within an English speaking community. Yet another context of immersion education is where the aim is to revive a lesser-used language. An example of this is the case of Irish in Ireland. Irish, one of the two official languages (with English) is spoken by a very small percentage of the population. In the Irish situation of language loss, immersion schools are one of the important elements in a revival of interest in the language. The first early Irish immersion school at kindergarten level was established in 1968. By 1993, there were one hundred and ninety kindergarten immersion schools in Irish (*naionrai*) (Hickey, 1998). Immersion education in Irish has since spread to elementary and secondary schools which are now immensely popular especially on the east coast of Ireland. Lastly, immersion education can be carried on in the language of power and prestige. In Singapore, for example, where the national language is Malay and the four official languages are Malay, English, Mandarin and Tamil, there are immersion schools in English. This is a case of subtractive bilingualism, where the first language is neglected in the school programs and the resources poured into the second language. English is cultivated as a *lingua franca* and used internationally.[6]

In Canada, immersion education has continued to flourish and expand in size as well as throughout different educational levels. Students can take immersion programmes in Canada from kinder- garten level through their university degree programme. As we have seen, similar highly successful immersion programmes have since been set up throughout the world. In addition, a large body of research now exists which has closely examined a great number of aspects of immersion education (Lambert and Tucker, 1972; Cummins and Swain, 1986; Genesee, 1987; Wesche, Morrison et al., 1990; Harley, 1993; Lyster, 1994; Johnson and Swain, 1997 and Swain, 2000; and many others). Immersion education has also been highlighted in the media. An underlying accepted notion in relation to immersion is that

5   For a discussion of restricted speakers see Mougeon and Beniak (2002).
6   For a fuller discussion of different models of bilingual education adapted by different groups in society to serve their own purposes see Swain (2000).

young children are predisposed to learn language through exposure to the language in subject-orientated contexts. This encouraged the setting up of early total immersion, where children at a young age are taught totally through French from kindergarten level.

According to Johnson and Swain (1997) the following features are typical of immersion programmes:

- the L2 is used as a medium of instruction in subject-matter classes
- the immersion curriculum (mathematics, science and geography, for instance) parallels the local L1 curriculum
- overt support exists for the L1, first and foremost in the form of positive attitudes towards it and also in the form of language arts instruction and often as a medium of instruction in subject-matter classes
- the programme aims for additive bilingualism so that, by the end, the L2 proficiency of immersion students is high, although not usually native-like, and their L1 proficiency is comparable to that of nonimmersion students who have followed the same curriculum in their L1
- exposure to the L2 is largely confined to the class-room
- students enter with similar (and limited) L2 proficiency
- the teachers are bilingual
- the classroom culture is that of the local L1 community

Total immersion is where one hundred percent of the subject matter is taught through the medium of the L2. This is generally the case only for two or three years, after which a proportion of subject matter is taught through the L1. *Partial immersion* means that a minimum of fifty percent of the material is taught through the L2.

Types of immersion: early, early double, delayed and late

Generally, immersion can be categorised as early, delayed (or middle) or late, in relation to the age at which immersion begins, as well as full or partial immersion in relation to the amount of instruction provided in French. In early full immersion the children, from kindergarten on, learn through the target language, French, throughout their full school day. In partial immersion, students are taught through the L2 for part of the school day and in their L1 for the rest of the day. Different subjects are taught in different languages. Language arts are taught in both languages.

In the Canadian educational system, early immersion happens in kindergarten or first grade (at about five years old), middle immersion in grades 4 or 5 (nine or ten years old approximately) and late immersion, in grades 6 to 8 (from about twelve years old). Both middle and late immersion have about 50% to 80% of instruction in French. Early double immersion refers to the situation where the child is exposed not to one other language but to two, in the same way. Genesee and Lambert (1983) describe such a case in Montreal, where English L1 Canadian children are taught through both French and Hebrew. The community added Hebrew as a religious and cultural part of its Jewish heritage. French is used to teach mathematics, science and social studies as well as language arts. Hebrew is used to teach language, history and religious and cultural studies. Otherwise double immersion is similar to regular immersion.

Immersion programmes are usually placed in dual track schools, which offer both immersion and non-immersion programmes. Immersion teachers are either L1 speakers of French or have near-native speaker proficiency. They use French only in the classroom and students are expected to use only French in their responses and inter-action in the classroom. After early immersion, a maintenance programme at some secondary schools sometimes provides further support for the language acquisition of the students. In delayed immersion where the child begins immersion at about ten years, either half or all of the instruction is provided in French. They normally have already had some exposure to French before beginning delayed immersion. Late immersion starts at the beginning of secondary school; again the children have already been exposed to varying amounts of French. All subjects, except for English language arts, are taught through French by L1 speakers or near-native speakers. The curriculum is the same as that of a non-immersion school and the immersion students are able to follow the same courses as native French speaking students. In general, there is much variation in the different components of immersion programmes throughout Canada; proportion of L2 used, proportion of early and late immersion, the subjects taught through the L2 and the number of immersion languages.

What we know about immersion education

The initial research on immersion programmes was again driven by parents, in the same way as the setting up of the programmes themselves. These parents needed to evaluate the results for their children of their experience in immersion education. They were concerned about the overall academic performance of their children in the programmes and wanted to know if their progress in other subjects would be impeded or slowed down in any way. They also wanted to know if their L1 English proficiency would suffer while the children were learning other subjects in the curriculum through the medium of French. And finally, they wanted to know if performance in L2 French actually was better than if the children had stayed in an English-medium school programme.

The results of all the research carried out on immersion programmes was reassuring and remains positive to this day (Swain, 2005). Parental concerns about immersion education were a factor in the chiefly outcome-focussed research which was carried out. However, recently there has been a move towards more process-focussed research. This places the learner at the centre of inquiry and ethnographic research highlights the experience of the learner during the process of acquisition in immersion (de Courcy, 2002).

Product-focussed research
on immersion programmes in Canada

The earlier outcome-focussed research found that there was no nega-tive effect on L1 development (Lambert and Tucker, 1972; Genesee, 1983; Cleghorn and Genesee, 1984; Genesee, Holobow et al., 1985; Genesee, 1987). The children, when tested on vocabulary, reading comprehension, spelling and writing, were found to be at least equal in standard to children in English medium schools. In fact, they did slightly better. In relation to knowledge of content, the children in immersion education were found again to be better than children in English-speaking classes (Krashen, 1984; Swain, 1985; Genesee, 1987). As regards L2 acquisition, the children from immersion programmes did significantly better than those who were not in im-mersion programmes. Genesee, Holobow et al. (1985) found that immersion students do as well as francophone students on listening and reading in French. And they do much better in French than those children in traditional French classes. However, Krashen and others found that the immersion learners were not fully native-like in terms of pronunciation and other language competences.

Comparisons were made in the research between early and late immersion students' performances. Day and Shapson (1988 and 1996) found that both early and later immersion students did well in French language in programmes in British Columbia. These students also did well on English reading, science and mathematics as compared with other students in non-immersion education. Early and late immersion learners in Ottawa were studied by Pawley (1986), who found that their French language proficiency, while not at a native level, was nevertheless high. However, the early immersion learners' rate was slightly higher than the late. Students in Manitoba were studied by Stennett and Earl (1983) at the end of their first year in a late im-mersion programme. They compared favourably with non-immersion students on tests of English reading comprehension, mathematics and IQ tests. Later, research began to focus on the learners themselves and began to use attitudinal questionnaires and participant observation in classrooms (Lapkin, Swain and Shapson, 1990).

Wesche, Morrison et al. (1990), at the University of Ottawa, studied students at four Canadian universities. They examined language proficiency, attitudes to French and how these students used French. They compared early and late immersion, students from various universities and students other than Ottawa students. They found that early immersion speakers did better than late on listening and speaking, but that there was no difference in their written performance. They also found that students at the University of Ottawa used French more than those at other universities and tended to take more courses in French. The University of Ottawa provides sheltered programmes which encourage the students to continue using French throughout their university careers. Olson (1983) focused his research on attitudes of parents of children in immersion programmes. The work is based on surveys. He found that immersion students were predominantly from middle class backgrounds and the motivation of parents was primarily to position their children for job opportunities. In general, he found immersion programmes to be elitist and that they attract the best students from English-medium education in Canada, to the detriment of the latter. However, Lapkin, Swain et al. (1990) and Lapkin (1998), while admitting the preponderance of middle class students in immersion education, point out that there is nevertheless a considerable number of children from working class backgrounds participating in immersion programmes.[7]

Social-psychological outcomes

Research has found (Genesee, 1987) that immersion students perceive less social difference between themselves and speakers of the L2 target. In addition, their perception of their L1 identity is as positive as that of non-immersion students. Immersion students have more positive attitudes toward the target language and the L2 speech community than non-immersion students. Of particular interest is the unusual

7   This is increasingly true of immersion elsewhere, for example in Ireland.

117

situation in Canada of Montreal, where comparative studies have been carried out between immersion and non-immersion students in relation to use of L2 French in the L1 speech community. Immersion students felt more comfortable and confident using French with francophone speakers, more likely to respond in French when addressed in French and less likely to avoid situations where French would be spoken. Many of the studies carried out on immersion and non-immersion students suggested that more contact with native speakers was necessary to develop further language proficiency.

Process-focussed research on immersion programmes in Canada

More recent research on language learning in an immersion setting has focussed more on the process of language acquisition than simply the product. de Courcy (2002) suggests that as long as initial concerns on the part of both parents and researchers about language development had been dealt with, researchers in immersion could now move on to focussing on the teaching/learning process.

Within the immersion classroom with the issue of both conveying content and language at the same time, specific strategies are necessary. With years of experience teachers have found that negotiating meaning leads to the provision of comprehensible input. A central theme in second language acquisition is that of input and interaction. *Input* as we have seen, is the language a learner hears or receives and from which they can learn. The language the learner produces after hearing input is called *output*. In L2 acquisition, *intake* is input which is helpful for the learner to internalise the language. Some of the input may be too rapid or difficult to understand and so is not useful for the learner for learning, that is, cannot serve as *intake*.

According to Krashen (1985) and others, L2 acquisition cannot take place without comprehensible input, and if lots of comprehensible input is provided then language acquisition happens.

118

Students don't simply learn the rule in the language class and have it 're-inforced' in the subject-matter class. The subject-matter class is a language class if it is made comprehensible to the language student. In fact the subject-matter class may even be better than the language class for language acquisition. (Krashen, 1984: 62)

However, it was found that simply providing comprehensible input was not sufficient to advance L2 acquisition. Output is necessary according to Swain (1985) and Chaudron (1986). Given what second language acquisition theory knows as the one-to-one principle (Andersen, 1984), the learner needs to be able to be made aware of form-to-function relationships in the acquisition process. In this way, the student can not only comprehend but also produce language in many different contexts. With this in mind, Lyster (1994), Met (1994), Rebuffot and Lyster (1996), Rebuffot (1998) and others have outlined methods for approaching L2 instruction in the classroom. A content-based approach focuses the attention on the language needed to learn the content which can later be expanded on in the language arts class. In addition, Harley (1994) shows that yet more attention needs to be paid to the less salient features of the second language. Harley (1993 and 1994) points out that communicatively-based activities in con-trived, yet meaningful, contexts are necessary. This allows the students to 'notice' and then use a wide range of features of which they might otherwise remain unaware. Many strategies can be used to provide such comprehensible input including repetition, redundancy, paraphrase, exemplification, slow rate of speech, use of less complex syntactic structures.

Interaction

Interaction involves amongst other areas, the sort of input modifica-tions which are made by native speakers when they address the L2 speaker. Studies on immersion learning within this framework measure and describe the behaviour of students and teachers in class-rooms, describe what happens during a lesson, study the relationship between teaching and learning, evaluate teaching and help improve the process of teaching. In interactionist analysis, classroom behaviour

119

is observed and different types of student and teacher activity are classified. The context of acquisition is considered an important factor. Much important theoretical work in this area has been produced, for example, by Long (1983), Pica and Doughty (1985), Pica (1988) and Long (2000).

Interactional modifications between native speakers (sometimes teachers) and non-native speakers include repetition, paraphrase, expansion and elaboration, sentence completion, comprehension check and requests for clarification. Immersion teachers have used to positive effect methods which take into account the implications of research on input and interaction. Long (1996) and others hold that interaction should be the central force in L2 pedagogy. In the immersion classroom, teacher-student interaction is a forum for providing corrective feedback in response to students' non-target utterances. A negotiation of outcome takes place in the interaction between student and teacher in the classroom, very much in the way this process takes place between native and non-native speakers in a naturalistic setting. It is thus that input can go from just being language as raw data to being made comprehensible. By the learner providing feedback (e.g., *Je ne comprends pas, Vous voulez répéter? la chose que vous portez à la tête*), he/she gradually matches the form to the meaning.

A classroom observation study was carried out in the context of the Development of Bilingual Proficiency project which is described in Swain and Lapkin (1989). The Communicative Orientation of Language teaching scheme observed nineteen early total immersion classrooms in Toronto and its suburbs. The project studied vocabulary instruction, *tu/vous* input (formal and informal address forms), error correction, and restricted/restrained talk by students. They found that vocabulary instruction was quite limited in the classroom. The students tended to learn only words as they arose in written texts and the use of these words in wider contexts was very little explored. They found in relation to *tu/vous* usage, that there was little or no use of *vous* in the input available to the students and as a consequence, they themselves used *tu* almost always, even to teachers who would require *vous* in native speaker speech for politeness sake. Error correction happened very rarely and then only in a confusing way. There was very little opportunity for sustained talk by the students. Discourse analysis revealed that mostly the students just briefly answered questions asked by the teacher. Carlson (1992) also used a discourse approach to examine patterns of teacher–student and student–teacher interaction. Froc (1995) described patterns of error correction in the immersion classroom. In general, it is not enough to provide positive responses to content answers. The student needs to have their attention drawn to their non-target utterances and to point up the links between form and meaning.

Lyster (1992 and 1994), with a rich background of classroom experience himself, made a study of the acquisition of sociolinguistic competence in French immersion programmes. This study focussed on the language used by the students. He observed how materials focussing on sociolinguistic awareness were used in the classroom. Then he tested the students to see whether the students were more sociolinguistically aware after use of the materials. He found a considerable change in the group which had used the materials. A benefit of this research is that it used both quantitative and qualitative data to investigate the process of language acquisition in the immersion classroom. Kowal and Swain (1997) describe how Kowal, also from a personal experience of the classroom, explored the students' thought processes in French immersion and tried, on this basis, to help the students with the L2 process. Barthomeuf (1991) did one of the rare studies on group activity in the immersion classroom. He investigated how children use language in a group and what sorts of activity could be observed. He found that the children used lots of the 'private speech' which has been seen to be very much part of the strategies used by immersion learners. Cleghorn and Genesee (1984) carried out an ethnographic study in an early French immersion school in Montreal. They investigated relationships between teachers, and between French immersion staff and the English staff. Another larger ethnographic study was carried out over two years in a French immersion kindergarten (Tardif and Weber, 1987). This explored the experience of the child in the immersion milieu and, in particular, how they made sense of what was going on in the L2 classroom. The authors conclude that the most important feature in working out how the children make sense of this situation is the interaction between teacher talk and student talk.[8]

The acquisition of sociolinguistic competence

Recently a new body of work has investigated the acquisition of sociolinguistic competence. The interest of this work for immersion education is that this area of language competence seems to be one which has been less successfully achieved in the immersion classroom so far. The Ministry of Education of Ontario, in its directives for the teaching of French in French immersion programmes specifies that by the end of their studies, students should be:

1. capable of using familiar and idiomatic phrases
2. able to express themselves using formal and informal registers
3. aware of nuances in different varieties of oral French
4. capable of identifying and understanding accents, lexical variation and varieties of continental and Canadian French.

As we saw earlier, while the performance of immersion students on skills such as speaking and writing is impressive – they score like native French speakers on listening and reading comprehension and use creative communicative strategies – nevertheless they are generally agreed to be not quite native-like in certain areas. One of these seems to be sociolinguistic competence (Swain and Lapkin, 1990). Lyster (1992 and 1994) focused on the effect of pedagogical materials in the immersion classroom in relation to sociolinguistic competence.

An important new body of work on immersion and the acquisition of sociolinguistic competence situates itself within a wider research programme which is quantitative and has a variationist

8   For a further account of the immersion literature see de Courcy (2002).

approach.[9] Mougeon and his colleagues (Mougeon and Rehner, 1998; Rehner and Mougeon, 1999; Mougeon, Nadasdi et al., 2001; Mougeon and Rehner, 2001; Mougeon, Nadasdi and Rehner, 2002; Nadasdi, Mougeon and Rehner, 2003; Rehner, Mougeon and Nadasdi, 2003; Mougeon, Rehner and Nadasdi, 2004; Mougeon, 2006) investigate the acquisition of sociolinguistic competence and in particular the acquisition of native speaker variation patterns by learners in immersion programmes in Canada.

This new research thread of variationist research in second language acquisition (Bayley and Regan, 2004) examines variability in L2 speech, as the learner moves from variability between two or more non-target forms to the use of only target forms. Recently researchers in this area have been examining the acquisition of variation as it happens in native speech. For instance, the native speaker in French will variably use *je sais pas* or *je ne sais pas*. The research of Mougeon and his colleagues examines precisely how these native speaker variation patterns are acquired by learners in the immersion classroom in Canada (Rehner, Mougeon et al., 2003, for instance). Mougeon and his colleagues investigate thirteen variables in spoken French as they are acquired by immersion students. They determine to what extent students in immersion programmes have acquired the variation patterns which characterise French in Canada, by reference to such questions as: Can the students emerging from immersion programmes interact appropriately with native speakers of Canadian French? Have they acquired native speaker variation as it relates to formal and informal occasions? They categorise the variables studied according to levels of formality and investigate the input the students receive from teaching materials and teacher speech.

Mougeon and his colleagues carried out fine-grained, quantitative variationist studies of the speech of the immersion learners using

9 'Variationist sociolinguistics is the tradition inspired by William Labov, which describes patterns and structures of language variation. Variationist approaches commonly adopt a quantitative methodology, focusing on the frequency with which linguistic forms (e.g. pronunciation or grammatical features) occur across speakers, groups of speakers or speaking styles.' (Swann, Deumert, Lillis and Mesthrie, 2004: 323)

a Varbrul analysis. Results of Varbrul analysis provide probability figures which give the likelihood of a variant being chosen by the speaker, given multiple linguistic and extra-linguistic factors. A detailed close-up picture of the L2 immersion language is provided by this analysis. On the whole the researchers found that immersion speakers tend to use vernacular variants less than native speakers do. For instance, in the case of *nous/on* alternation, immersion students use the standard variant in 44% of occurrences compared to 1% for native speakers and for *ne* usage, the standard variant is used 70% by immersion students, while native speakers use it at only 0.5%. Mougeon and his colleagues conclude that this is due to lack of prolonged contact with native speakers. This is confirmed in relation to Canadian French by the work of Nagy, Blondeau and Auger (2003) who also, using variationist analysis, found that those anglophone speakers who lived in the native speech community, as in Montreal for instance, used native speech variation patterns and native speaker rates of variants much more than immersion speakers and by other Varbrul studies in relation to the acquisition of continental French (Regan, 1995, 1996 and 1998; Dewaele and Regan, 2001).

Conclusions to be drawn perhaps are that immersion learners, who are already at an extremely high proficiency level from their prolonged immersion experience, could benefit even further from home stays in francophone families in Quebec, for instance, which have already been found to have positive effects in the acquisition of sociolinguistic competence (Lapkin, Hart and Swain, 1995). Freed, Segalowitz and Dewy (2004) found, in relation to American students of French L2, that fluency increased significantly in an intensive domestic immersion context of acquisition where the classroom immersion experience was complemented by:

> [...] daily opportunities to use French through participation on a soccer team, in a French School choir, and in painting classes, weekly musical performances, films and a cabaret offered on a regular basis. Enhancing these activities were frequent trips (e.g. to Montreal), parties, and cultural events to promote awareness of a diverse Francophone culture and the development of French language skills'. (Dewy, 2004: 282)

However, it seems that it is not sufficient to conclude that simply being in the native speech community is enough to necessarily enhance proficiency. Stays in the target language community can vary considerably according to the degree of contact with native speakers which is available to the learners and which is equally sought by the learner (see, for instance, Regan, 1995, 1996 and 1997; Wilkinson, 1998). However, research has shown that, on the whole, such stays in the speech community, provided there is reasonable contact with native speakers, seem to enhance sociolinguistic competence at least, if not other areas of L2 acquisition as well (Wesche, Morrison et al., 1990; Wesche 1993).

Long-term effects of immersion

What about the long term effects of immersion programmes on the lives of those who experience them? What about the effects on university education, and especially on entry into the workplace? Immersion education has been a resounding success in every way in which the parents of the 1960s hoped. In terms of general effects, immersion provides the closest possible alternative to a naturalistic context for acquisition while remaining within a classroom. Content is successfully taught and the children are academically on target. In addition, the psycho-social effects are positive in relation to the students' attitudes to the French language and the native-speaking community.

Research on long term effects of the immersion experience is less extensive than that on effects in the shorter term. Wesche (1993) carried out studies on the graduates from immersion programmes, studying two cohorts of Ottawa area French immersion graduates. The studies were longitudinal and replicated earlier studies. Research questions were:

- What can the students do in French at the end of high school?
- What can they do at the end of undergraduate studies?
- How well can they write in French at the end of high school?
- Has their English development been affected?
- Does an early (kindergarten) versus a later (grade 6/7 starting age make a long-term difference?
- How do they feel about using French in their daily lives?
- What do they actually DO in French?
- Has immersion made a difference to their ethnolinguistic attitudes?
- What are their attitudes toward immersion schooling?

The subjects were graduates of bilingual high schools in the Ottawa region attending nearby universities: the bilingual University of Ottawa, which attracts the largest number, with a mixed anglophone and francophone student body and a wide range of undergraduate and graduate programmes in French; Carleton University, an English language university also in Ottawa; the English-language Queen's University, in Kingston, and McGill University, an English-language university with some French programmes in mainly French-speaking Montreal. The subjects were interviewed on entry to university, after three years at university and also after finishing university. In fact there was a post-university study, with most respondents having full-time jobs and a few pursuing graduate studies. The majority lived in the Ottawa area. Most show no significant difference from the fuller sample taken during university studies. The results of the two studies can be summarised in very general terms.[10] Many of the outcomes noticed had already been noticed and reported in earlier studies of the immersion programmes in process. Some however relate especially to long-term outcomes.

10   They are presented in greater detail in Swain and Lapkin (1989) and Lapkin (1998).

- High levels of functional L2 ability can be achieved by language majority children through L2 medium schools.
- Immersion L2 skills acquired through communicative use over many years are robust and are maintained for long periods, even in the absence of frequent use.
- Even among the strongest students, immersion schooling alone does not develop native-like L2 users except on global comprehension skills involving 'school' language. Gaps are apparent in grammar, vocabulary range and precision and familiarity with varied discourse domains. Graduates can, however, manage in their L2 in most situations, including post-secondary study in French. The native-like L2 skills of Anglophone graduates of francophone schools suggests that lack of interaction with native peers is an important factor in the non-native immersion outcomes.
- An intensive L2 dose and use of the L2 as an instructional medium are essential features of immersion; an early start is not. However, graduates overwhelmingly favour an early start.
- Immersion graduates show very high levels of satisfaction with their immersion experience.

Individual differences in proficiency, attitudes and French use among immersion graduates are striking, indicating, according to Wesche, that instructed exposure is not the only variable. She maintains that it is unrealistic to expect graduates to seek personal and cultural contact with the L2 groups on the basis of a basically school-bound programme, and points out that there may be things which we cannot achieve in school or at least which will not be learned 'incidentally'. The evidence from the study suggests importantly that out-of-class activity in the L2 and contact with native speakers during immersion study are linked both to proficiency development and the greater use of the language in later life, and that early contact is particularly linked to a more integrative orientation toward speakers of the L2, their culture and L2 use. Wesche concludes that in relation to immersion's broader socio-political implications 'if the immersion language learning experience remains essentially school-bound and contact of most graduates with Francophones and their culture remains infrequent these may [...] be more limited than had been expected.' (Wesche, 1993: 232–233)

Harley (1994) carried out a study which examined the issue of immersion graduates' preparedness for the workplace. She looked at one private sector position, the nature of its language requirements and the ability of immersion graduates to meet those requirements. She found that many immersion graduates from English speaking areas probably have the French language skills necessary to hold this position. In addition, the kinds of bilingual jobs on offer revealed a mismatch between immersion students' career aspirations and the entry-level nature of the bilingual positions for which they may be qualified after their secondary education plus some undergraduate training. Mougeon (2006) asks the question: How much French is enough for a given workplace?

Probably the most recent work on long term effects of immersion education is Mougeon's study of immersion secondary students' experience at university (Mougeon, 2006). This study provides a follow-up to previous studies by Mougeon et al. on the acquisition of sociolinguistic competence by immersion students at secondary level. This study investigated the use of *nous/on* alternation in the speech of thirty-two immersion students (elementary and secondary) and forty-nine core French and regular school students. Interviews and question-naires were used to examine the use of this variable in the speech of the students. The research questions were: Do students continue to acquire and use sociolinguistic variants through university? If not, which factors, linguistic and extra-linguistic, affect their usage? Factors hypothesised to affect usage included: year, age, sex, parents' level of education, first language, home language and length of time in Study Abroad/Home Stays. First person plural pronouns were con-sidered for reference to specificity and restriction, and non restriction. The variant *on* is the preferred one by L1 speakers (Blondeau, 2002) for French Canadian speakers and Coveney (2000) for continental French speakers.

A GoldVarb analysis[11] found that the former immersion speakers used *on* 87% of the time. This was a higher figure than that of Mougeon in relation to the immersion students while they were at secondary level. Now, at university, they seem to be using more of the vernacular variant. Mougeon suggests that affecting factors may include the fact that the students are now older, they have more contact with L1 speakers or it may have to do with their choosing a bilingual university (where *on* may be used by faculty members). Mougeon found that the effect of interaction was very strong. Extra-curricular activities were an important factor in *on* usage. In particular, a stay in the native speech community of longer than three months was a strong influencing factor. This confirms much research which shows that contact with the native speech community and long-term stays in the community may well be the most important factors in acquiring sociolinguistic competence (for instance, Mougeon and Beniak 1981 and 1991; Regan, 1995; Dewaele and Regan, 2001). Mougeon's overall conclusions were that exposure to native speaker speech seems to reinforce the acquisition of vernacular speech which was begun during immersion education at primary and secondary level. However usage does not change from year 1 at university to year 4, unless the speakers are frequent users of French. Where progression from years 1 to 4 made no difference, stays in the community markedly affected use of L1 speech variants.

11   GoldVarb is a version of the computer program developed to analyse statistic-ally variation in language. Prototypically these methods involve the use of the computer program known as VARBRUL to analyse the social and linguistic distribution of variant linguistic forms in terms of variable rules. For more comprehensive accounts of variationist analysis see, for example, Labov (1994 and 2001), Guy (1995), Poplack and Tagliamonte (2001) Sankoff and Labov (1979).

Conclusion

Perhaps what is most striking about French immersion programs is that in the light of the fragile position of French in Canada, immersion education seems to offer a clear hope and possibilities for the future of French, certainly in relation to Canada outside Quebec. Research has found that the most 'bilingual' period in the linguistic life of anglophone speakers is during adolescence in immersion secondary education (see Chapter 4). This would certainly underline what we know to be the significant advantages of immersion education in the acquisition and use of French. It seems that, second only to living in the native speech community and having significant contact with native speakers, classroom immersion French education offers a distinct support to the position of French in Canada. (As indeed we saw earlier was the case for the acquisition of Swedish in Finland.) Indeed there are currently initiatives taking place in the education system in the immersion project which, taking recent research into account, are considering how best to incorporate means of providing the learner with the closest possible model of spontaneous speech of the native speech community.

6   Which French?
Language contact, variation and change

Introduction: variability in Canadian French

Canadian French since the Quiet Revolution, and especially in the past few decades, has asserted itself confidently as a variety of French equal to French in the Hexagon, Belgium, Switzerland and other regional varieties. From a previous position of linguistic insecurity, French Canada is increasingly taking a lead role internationally in language planning in relation to French. An example of this increased standing of Canadian French is the admiration in which it is held in France for its stated firm stand in relation to anglicisms. In this new linguistic confidence, Canadian speakers have been significantly helped by provincial legislation which underpinned the status of French in Quebec and federal legislation which established the position of French in Canada (the Official Languages Act 1969, where English and French were accorded equal status and in Quebec with Bill 101 or the Charter of the French Language which only recognises French as the official language of the province; see earlier this volume). Nevertheless Canadian French is very much a distinctive variety of French and very much part of Canadian identity. This identity is bound up with its long standing contact with English. However, the language contact situation of French and English is by no means a simple one. In order to discuss language change and development in French Canada, we must also explore the extent to which French is affected by its relationship with English.

There is a very rich body of sociolinguistic research relating to Canadian French. The earliest work of this type was begun with the Montreal corpus of French (Sankoff and Vincent, 1980, Sankoff and Cedergren, 1973) which examined a stratified sample of speakers ranged according to age, sex and social class. Correlations were found between variable features in French and these extra-linguistic factors. Sociolinguistic research was also carried out in Quebec City (Deshaies, 1981) and on Ontario French (Mougeon, Brent-Palmer et al., 1982) and in the 1980s Poplack's Ottawa-Hull corpus looked at French in the Ottawa area (Poplack, 1989). Further sociolinguistic corpora were established for the Atlantic provinces in which French is spoken: New Brunswick, Nova Scotia (Flikeid, 1989), and Newfoundland (King, 1994).

To describe Canadian French, we need to examine and understand variation in the language. For many linguists, language is, by its very nature, inherently variable. Sociolinguists, particularly variationist sociolinguists, hold that variation goes deep into the grammar of language and that any adequate explanation of language involves an account of variability (Weinreich, Labov and Herzog, 1968; Labov, 1994, 2001). Variation in any language exists in time and space, and reflects both geographical as well as social influences. Some of the factors that influence variability include the region the speaker comes from, the age of the speaker, gender, socio-economic standing. Variation frequently indicates change and for this reason, it is important to understand variation if we are to see future directions for the language. The sociolinguistic body of work which has been done on the French of Canada has explored the varieties of French in Canada and many variables in vernacular speech in Canada, some of which are undergoing change.

Variation and change

In a situation of potential change, where there are two or more forms referring to the same thing, one form being new, a contest frequently takes place where one form finally wins out and becomes the accepted form in the speech community. However, variability (that is, more than one form referring to the same thing) does not always necessarily mean change. For instance, in variants of English all over the world, the alternate forms *ing* and *in,* as in *walking* and *walkin'* have existed since Shakespeare's time, at least, and continue to exist as a choice for today's speaker, who is more or less likely to use one form instead of the other depending on certain factors. These are linguistic and extra-linguistic factors such as context (formal or informal), gender of the speaker, age of the speaker, social class of the speaker and linguistic factors such as the previous sound, grammatical category and so on; all of these factors may influence choice between variant forms without any consequent long-term linguistic change.

While it is true that variability does not inevitably mean change, it very often does suggest a change in progress, where one form may be in the process of being lost. Frequently the speech of young people is an indication of the direction the language is taking, as is also the speech of younger women who are frequently found to be innovators in speech change. *Ne* deletion in negation in Canadian French is an example of variability which may well indicate a change in progress, where, in the future, the language may no longer use the first particle of negation *ne* but express it by the current second particle *pas*. /l/ deletion is another such example, where variable usage in the present looks as if /l/ in personal pronouns and clitics[1] may well disappear from the language. The pronunciation of /r/ is another item which looks as if it is undergoing change in several varieties of French in Canada: where older people use a flap or a trill, younger people are using a uvular /r/ as in Standard European French. Many of the speech forms which are undergoing change in Canadian French are those which are similarly undergoing such evolution in European French. In the context of changes taking place in all variants of French, Canadian French is further advanced in the progress of these and certain other variables than Standard European French. Many vernacular variants have been studied in the various corpora above and in many cases, the same ones have been studied in different speech communities and compared. In several instances, recent revisitings have been carried out of the original corpora and thus changes have been charted between the speech of the 1970s and recent usages (Blondeau, 2001).

As noted, variation does not always mean change and sometimes variation is incorrectly presumed to indicate change. In the case of French Canada, this is further complicated by controversy regarding

---

1   A clitic is a grammatical form which cannot stand on its own; for example in *il va*, *il* is a clitic.

the impact of English regarding change in French. It is often presumed that some of the variants observed in French are the result of recent changes which reflect the influence of English, but recent research has shown how complex the relation between French and English is in Canada. Many vernacular forms in Canadian French which are generally denigrated and presumed to be due to the influence of contact with English, are in fact, part of the pattern of variation which has existed for centuries in vernacular speech. In this chapter, we will describe the characteristics of Canadian French, including some of the variable elements which give it its particular 'colour'. We will discuss those elements which are variable and may indicate the direction which the language will take in the future in Canada, and we will discuss the effects of language contact, which, it transpires, are more complex than first appears.

Language contact: change, borrowing, code-switching

Canada is a country of multiple languages co-existing and inter-weaving with each other and affecting each other in multiple ways. The study of language contact is a highly developed field within linguistics; among the many accounts of language contact are: Poplack (1980), Grosjean (1982), Silva-Corvalan (1986), Myers-Scotton (1993), Milroy and Muysken (1995), Poplack and Meechan (1998), Thomason (2001), Mougeon and Beniak (2002), and Sankoff (2002). French and English in Canada have been in a classic language contact situation in relation to each other for centuries; in relation to the contact situation in Canada in particular, see, for example, Poplack (1988) and Swann, Deumert et al. (2004: 167–168). In general, research in language contact studies how languages mix due to contact. Swann, Deumert et al. (2004) define language contact as:

> The co-existence of languages in a geographical area or in a speech community.
> A degree of bilingualism is usually involved, either throughout the speech
> community or on the part of some individuals. The field of language contact is

concerned with macrosociolinguistic issues like language maintenance and language shift, as well as microsociolinguistic issues like the effects of borrowing, code-switching.

Every language changes over time; this is inevitable and will take place even if there is no contact with other languages. French in France, for instance is changing. Indeed, some of the changes observed in Canadian French are also taking place in other French speaking areas. Change can be due to multiple factors. In the case of Canada, there is also change due to contact with English, Amerindian languages and, increasingly, other languages. It may be difficult to distinguish between internal change and contact induced change. Furthermore, in Canada, the issue of language change can be controversial. Change is sometimes ascribed to contact, with insufficient evidence. Various French–English contact situations in Canada have been studied from various angles such as the grammatical effects of contact (Poplack, Sankoff and Miller, 1988), pragmatic issues (King and Nadasdi, 1999) and the effects of language contact on the minority language (Beniak, Mougeon et al., 1985).

One indication of language change due to contact is the use of words from other languages. This involves both borrowing and code-switching. Borrowing occurs when a vocabulary item from one language is introduced into another language. This implies re-arrangement of elements in the language. This rearrangement is not a haphazard process; it has been found to take place in a principled way. For instance, if a language is 'missing' a word, we could view this as a 'gap' in the pattern. This 'gap' in the language then constitutes an ideal location for a borrowing to take place, and so then we see the language borrowing from the other language. There is then a re-arrangement of the structures and elements as the word is integrated into the host language. A word from English in Canada, for instance, may be borrowed into French and take on the phonological and morphological characteristics of French and thus become integrated into French. Borrowings may be only momentary ones or they may be integrated and become more permanent in the language and actually part of the system. One might conclude, on making a contrastive analysis of two languages and from the structures of both, that the reasons for borrowing are strictly language internal. However, this is not the case. Even in cases where there are good structural reasons for borrowing, it very often does not happen. In fact, borrowings are mediated by the socio-cultural setting of the contact situation. There are in fact many extra-linguistic factors which play a role in borrowing, whether on an individual or a group level. Such issues as the ability of the speaker to keep the languages separate, whether the individual wishes or needs to keep the languages separate, the proficiency of the speaker – the more proficient the speaker in the L2 the more likely they are to borrow. For a full account of borrowing and code-switching, see Poplack (1980).

Code-switching is another very common phenomenon where languages are in contact. Code-switching refers to instances when speakers switch between codes (language, or language varieties) in the course of a conversation. Switches may involve different amounts of speech and different linguistic units; clauses or simply words. In a study of French speakers in both Ottawa (Ontario) and Hull (Quebec), Poplack (1988) finds interesting differences in the uses of code-switching in the speech of the two communities. The two communities had different attitudes to code-switching, due in large part to their own attitudes to their own linguistic usage. The Hull speakers were more subject to linguistic insecurity than their counterparts in Ottawa and felt that they did not speak 'good' French – this chiefly in relation to Standard French of France. The Ottawa speakers code-switched to find the 'best' way of saying something; finding the *mot juste*. The Hull speakers switched for metalinguistic commentary, showing full awareness of using English. The upper middle-class speakers in Hull used this strategy for a third of all the data, where the working-class speakers showed an intermediate pattern. Poplack concludes: 'The Hull speakers' linguistic behavior is also consistent with their own favorable attitudes towards proper speech, their belief that inter-ventions from English are due to momentary lapses, as well as their attitude that good French must of necessity exclude anglicisms (Poplack and Meechan, 1998: 53). In general, Poplack found that the Ottawa Hull speakers have particular characteristics not necessarily found in the code-switching habits of other bilingual speakers. They 'draw attention to their code-switches by repetition, hesitations, intonational highlighting, explicit metalinguistic commentary etc, and use the contrast between the codes to underline the rhetorical appropriateness of their speech' (Poplack and Meechan, 1998: 53).

Contact-induced language change can be due to a multiplicity of reasons both linguistic and social. The social factors are receiving attention only relatively recently, for instance (Thomason, 2001: 60–61). Social factors include intensity of contact, proficiency of the speaker (the more proficient the speaker is in the L2 the more likely s/he is to use it) attitude of speakers, setting in which the language is being used (French speakers tend to use French in the home and family setting and English for more official public domains), functions for which the language is being used (the speaker may associate one language with certain functions rather than the other) or even whether the learner was a naturalistic or a formal/classroom learner of the language. Group level factors include the size of the groups of speakers of each language, the homogeneity of the groups, the prestige of each language, the degree of tolerance towards mixing. Prescriptive attitudes towards mixing also play a role in interference between the languages. In Canada, this tends to be relatively strong and normative statements on borrowing are regularly issued by various official language bodies. Linguistic factors include issues of markedness[2] and typological similarity between the languages. Mechanisms of contact induced change may include code-switching, code-mixing and borrowings. Mougeon and his colleagues have made an important analysis over many years of the effects of bilingualism and language restriction.[3]

In general, it seems that certain characteristics are common in cases of language contact where there is language restriction in the 'minority' language, minority meaning either 'a language whose speakers are socio-economically disadvantaged with respect to those of a 'superordinate' language, but also in a demographic sense, i.e. a language whose speakers are in numerical inferiority in comparison

2   Markedness is a rather vague concept in linguistics referring to both ease and frequency of a form; a linguistic item which is both frequent in the languages of the word and relatively 'easy', is said to be 'unmarked'.

3   For a further discussion, for example, see Mougeon and Beniak (2002: 1).

with those of a 'majority' language' (Mougeon and Beniak, 2002: 1–2). Among the features which are noticed to be characteristic of restricted language are simplification, reduction and interference. Weinreich's use of the term 'interference' (Weinreich, 1968), implies the influence of one linguistic system on another. Mougeon and Beniak use interference as a general term for all types of interlingual influence and they cite Weinreich's definitions:

> The practice of alternately using two languages will be called *bilingualism,* and the persons involved, *bilingual.* Those instances of deviation from the norms of either language which occur in the speech of bilinguals as a result of their familiarity with more than one language, i.e. as a result of language contact, will be referred to as *interference* phenomena. It is these phenomena of speech, and their impact on the norms of either language exposed to contact, that invite the interest of the linguist. (Mougeon and Beniak, 2002: 2)

The literature on language death (Dorian, 1981) shows that lack of exposure to and use of a language lead to changes such as loss of features or simplification. This can be due not only to interference but also to internal restructuring. Sociolectal reduction[4] has also been noted as a result of minority-language restriction (Poplack, 1997). Access to the appropriate social contexts in which the necessary input would be accessible may also be a problem for acquisition (as indeed it is crucial for all L2 learners). Restriction may result in a lack of knowledge of stylistic variation which would be common to non-restricted speakers. As we saw in Chapter 5, immersion speakers, who are agreed to be restricted speakers and who learn mostly formal French in school, generally tend to lack the ability to switch easily from formal registers to the more vernacular non-standard varieties of French.

In relation to speakers of Ontario French, Mougeon and Beniak (1991) studied the relationship between French language restriction and linguistic outcomes. They found, in keeping with other findings that morphosyntactic simplification, interference, and monostylism (in

---

4   Sociolectal reduction can be loosely defined as an insufficient knowledge of the range of sociolinguistic features which a native speaker has recourse to and which restricted speakers tend not to possess.

the speech of Franco-Ontario speakers there was limited use of the vernacular features of French) were the major characteristics. They suggest an implicational hierarchy, in addition, for the features: lexical borrowing is most pervasive throughout the whole speech community; next comes interference; then comes structural simplification and finally, least pervasive, is sociolectal reduction and '*calques*'.

Theoretical positions on the transfer of grammatical structure vary widely. It is certain that issues of interference and transfer are of crucial importance in relation to many structural aspects of languages in contact. However, in relation to certain aspects, recent socio-linguistic research suggests that the mechanisms of language contact induced process have been overstated in relation to varieties of French in Canada outside Quebec. Variationist research carried out by Poplack and her team has pinpointed instances where variation thought to be due to contact with English is in fact due to internal change in French. It is in fact frequently related to the gulf between prescriptive norms and actual usage on the part of speakers in the speech community. This research takes as axiomatic that study of the structural properties of language alone cannot explain language transfer. The direction and extent of interference, as well as the kinds of features transferred are socially determined (see Poplack, 1983, 1988, 1990; Poplack and Turpin, 1999; Poplack and Dion, 2004). For example, Poplack has carried out studies on a large database of spontaneous speech from the French speaking community in Ottawa-Hull (Leroux, 2003, 2004; Poplack and Dion, 2004). She examined, for example, the use of the subjunctive and the future temporal reference system in this speech community. The bilingual speakers are 'typical' language contact speakers who engage in lexical borrowing, code-switching and mixing. However the detailed, empirical quantitative studies did not find any replacement of French structures in relation to the use of the subjunctive by English-like features. In relation to future expression, Poplack found that the speakers variably used the periphrastic future (*je vais aller*), the inflected future (*j'irai*) and present-tense forms. In fact there is a significant change in progress in relation to future tense in the French of Ottawa speakers where the inflected future is in the process of being lost. (It is now used almost solely in a negative context.) In the language contact literature this had been reported as simplification due to transfer from English. Poplack however, finds that the use of the periphrastic form, the widespread form used, is, in fact, a language change which has been on-going for centuries in actual speech usage rather than what is prescribed by normative bodies (Poplack, 2001). In relation to the use of the subjunctive, again strictly prescribed for particular contexts by prescriptive grammarians, detailed, fine-grained, empirical variationist studies have revealed that there is in fact no change in usage attributable to contact with English.

In addition, this on-going research is showing that somewhat alarmist reports of wholesale borrowings from English are at times exaggerated (LeBlanc, 2002; Poplack and St-Amand, 2002). Diachronic evidence is currently being brought to bear on the issue (Poplack, 1998). Poplack posits that it is precisely the lack of reliable diachronic evidence on the spoken language which gives rise to the very general assumption that stigmatized features of contemporary vernaculars are recent innovations and due mainly to the influence of English. Using the data of corpora representing the spoken language of at least a century and a half ago, it becomes clear that speakers were indeed using those same non-prescriptive forms at least as far back as the nineteenth century.

Language change is an important issue in Canada because French is seen to be under threat by English. In fact, there is a range of reasons for language change. Some change is due to internal change and is taking place regardless of amount or type of language contact, while other change is taking place due to contact. Further, there is some variation in language which is presumed to be a consequence of language contact when it is simply the variability that has existed for many centuries. Social beliefs about language colour our knowledge of actual variation and change to such an extent that it is very difficult to separate ideology from fact.

Features of Canadian French

Whatever about language change and future directions, a description of current variation is important as a basis for predicting and accounting for such future change. Certain distinct features are seen as characteristic of the variety of 'Canadian French' (a generalising term which usually refers to a standard urban variety). Underlying much of the variation in Canadian French is the origin of the speakers who came mainly from two different colonies: one established by Champlain in 1604 at Port-Royal (Nova Scotia) and which was called Acadie, and the second colony four years later at Quebec. These two colonies gave rise to the two principal dialects of French in Canada: Acadian French and Quebec French. For a more detailed discussion of the origins of differences in the varieties see Conrick (2002b). Other varieties of French (Ontario, Michiff) derive from population movements within Canada.

These general features of Canadian French are often what speakers of other dialects of French perceive as salient when they listen to Canadian French:

Phonology
- the affrication of dental plosives before close front vowels: for example *tu* is pronounced [tsy] and *dis* pronounced [dzi]
- the elision of /l/ and /r/ with vowel lengthening, e.g., *suc(re)*
- the opening of vowels in closed syllables, with elision of vowels in polysyllabic words, e.g., toute [tʊt], difficile [dzifɪsɪl]
- diphthongisation of long vowels e.g., chose [ʃɔwz]
- /wa/ – /we/, moi becomes moe

Morphology
- general tendency to regularisation
- regularisation of plural markers: *cheval – chevals*
- extension of auxiliary *avoir* to all verbs in perfect tense
- levelling of vocalic alternation in present tense, e.g., *bois – boivons*
- the feminisation of professions: *professeure*

Syntax

- use of emphatic particle *là* [lɑ] suffixed to a phrase or clause and pronounced with a lower tone, e.g., *icit- là*
- use of periphrastic verb phrases, e.g., *être à faire* for European French *en train de faire*
- use of interrogative marker *ti* in questions, e.g., *où c'est-ti que tu vas?*
- word order in imperatives e.g. *dis-moi-le-pas*[5]

Lexis

Blanc (1993) gives examples of archaisms, neologisms, especially from scientific and technological domains, anglicisms from English loan words such as; *fun, chum, gang, brakes* or calques, for example; *fin de semaine, chien chaud, annonces classées* compared to *week end, hot dog, petites annonces* in European French. Lexis in Canadian French is particularly rich in swear words based on religious vocabulary: *calice, Christ, ciboire, hostie, sacrement, tabernacle.* These can also be strung together, (*hostie de criss de ciboire de tabernak!*). In many cases, words or expressions which disappeared in France continued in Canada, particularly those which existed before the Revolution in 1789 (archaisms). The language is also influenced by borrowings from Amerindian languages and the effects of English.

---

5   Adapted from Blanc (1993) who rightly points out that many of these features which are frequently taken to be specifically Canadian forms are actually also found in varieties of popular French in France such as *al or a* for *elle* (*elle me voit - a me voit*).

Varieties of Canadian French

There are several varieties of Canadian French, each with its own character. Quebec is in a French majority situation for instance, while Ontario French is found in areas where English may be dominant and so French is more under threat, and French beyond Ontario is heavily influenced by Cree and other Amerindian languages. The greatest difference between varieties of French in Canada, as we have seen, is due to the fact that over half of the Acadians came from south of the Loire whereas half of the Québécois came from north of the Loire. Both were later influenced by normative influences from within Canada itself, as well as by Canadian English. Quebec French is the variety of French as used within the limits of the province of Quebec in Canada. Acadian is spoken in the Atlantic provinces of Canada and is depicted in the writings of novelist Antonine Maillet. There are both similarities and differences between these two varieties of Canadian French on the level of phonology, grammar and lexis and so Quebec and Acadian French can be considered to be two separate varieties of Canadian French. For instance, *joual* (from *cheval*) a working-class variety, is part of Quebec French and is not found in Acadian.

Quebec

Many descriptions and dictionaries of Quebec French have been made from within various linguistic paradigms (Santerre, 1990; Picard, 1992; Boulanger, 1993; Léard, 1995; Barbaud, 1997; Plourde, 2000; Dostie, 2005; Heller, 1998; Gervais, 2003; Lockerbie, Molinaro et al., 2005). The major characteristics of the French language used in Quebec usually refer to archaisms, innovations and borrowings as typical features. Like any other linguistic variety, Quebec French varies with factors such as social class, age, gender, neighbourhood, rural vs. urban setting and the type of context, topic, and interlocutor.

Middle class speech differs from working class speech. *Joual* is the most stigmatised version of working class speech. In fact, since the Quiet Revolution there has been a renewed interest and pride in this particular variety which was known ever more widely due to its representation in the creative writing of Michel Tremblay, novels as well as theatre. Rural speech in Quebec tends to be archaic, while urban speech is more open to the influence of English. Quebec speakers can switch back and forth from the standard to the vernacular as they accommodate to one group or another.

Standard Quebec French

Related to the linguistic nationalism that accompanied the Quiet Revolution of the 60s, Standard Québécois French (a prestige variety) began to entrench itself firmly. This movement was related to the parallel emergence of a young Québécois middle class which emerged from its traditional domination by the Catholic Church, became a confident, outward-looking society and began to compete with its anglophone peers for control of the province's commercial and industrial sectors. It was felt that a standard French would aid in this enterprise, so that many of the older rural forms were excluded from this new standard Canadian French. In fact, standard Quebec French is relatively similar to French in France. And *Joual,* while it is seen as relatively stigmatised, is also similar in ways to many working class varieties of European French, for example, vernacular French spoken in Paris, other parts of France, or other European countries. One of many features of contemporary spoken language which are common both in Europe and in North America, for instance, is /r/ and /l/ deletion in final consonant clusters. Quebec French is most distinct from other varieties of French in its phonology and lexis. Features can be divided into those which have descended directly from seventeenth century French from France which have stayed the same in Canada and developed in different directions in France on the one hand, and on the other, are features which have developed within Canada.

The issue of linguistic norms plays an important part in the public debate on language in Canada. It has been a common theme since the establishment of the Société du parler français au Canada, dedicated to the study of the French language in Canada in 1902 (Verreault, Mercier and Lavoie, 2006), and continuing to this day (Lapierre, 1997). Much has been written and debated about how French should be spoken and written in Canada. This has specially manifested itself in debates about pedagogical norms – the issue of 'which' French should be taught in schools (Heller, 1998; Valdman, 1998; Auger and Valdman, 1999).

Archaisms

Archaisms are characteristic of Quebec French. These are the forms, as we have seen, which are descended from seventeenth century French. Examples of these are: *gadelle* from Normandy, *castille* from Poitou, *abrier, s'abrier* (compared to Hexagon French *couvrir and s'abriter.*) *Moe* instead of *moi,* /mwa/, used to be the standard pronunciation in French until the French Revolution. It has disappeared in Standard French in France but is still present in Canadian French.

Neologisms

In the enterprise of adapting and surviving in the new environment in which the early settlers found themselves, account needed to be taken by the language of their physical environment, their new social structures, legal and economic; new words had to be created or borrowed to fit the new extra-linguistic realities which the speakers were confronting daily. Words were created to refer to new plants, animals, agricultural and economic activities. Many of the terms in Quebec French which are different from those of France relate to a particularly Canadian environment: winter, the maple syrup industry, geographical terrain, Canadian seasons, and dramatically changing temperatures; words such as *capot, carriole, tuque, portage, poudrerie,* for fine snow in a blizzard, *sucrerie, banc de neige, huard, sapinage, attisée, bucher* meaning to cut up wood, *calé* for *chauve* (bald), *garrocher* meaning 'to throw', *corder* to pile up wood, *le solage* meaning the foundations of a house. Other neologisms were created to deal with economic development in Canada: *acériculture* for the industry which grew up around maple syrup, *aluminerie* for the production of aluminium, *avionnerie* for airplane construction and so on. Quebec French has a strong tendency to prefer neologisms to using English borrowings, as French does: instead of *ferry-boat, traversier* is used in Quebec; *salle de quilles* for *bowling, stationnement* for *parking, magasinage* for *shopping, escalier mobile* for *escalator, jardinière* for *garden center, légère* for *light* in relation to food, drinks and so on.

Recently, technology has contributed to the introduction of many new words into Quebec French. The word *logiciel* for instance, was introduced by the Québécois. The following terms for cyber space are among those which have also been introduced by Québécois speakers: *argent électronique,* (where the French say *electronic cash) babillard électronique (bulletin board system) café électronique (internet café), coup de feu (flame), fichier joint (attachment), forum de discussion (electronic discussion group), gratuiciel (freeware), outil de recherche (search engine), page d'accueil (home page), partagiciel (shareware), pirate informatique (hacker), clavardage (chat session), télécharger (download or upload), la Toile (le Web).* It is an indication of the concern about language contact in Canada that such terms have been created. In contrast, in France, speakers tend to borrow English technology terms.

The concern to distinguish French from English in Canada may also explain some innovations. The feminisation of titles has provided another source of innovations in Quebec French. The Office de la langue française of Quebec province decided in the 1980s that feminine forms had to be created for every professional title whose form was clearly masculine; for instance, *professeure, agente, écrivaine, présidente* (see Conrick, 1998, Bouchard et al, 1999; Niedzwiecki, 2002). These new forms are used at all levels of Quebec French including the most informal types of social settings, and represent a usage that is not only new but which does not exist to the same extent in other French-speaking areas.

Borrowings

Borrowings from Amerindian Languages
French was in a situation of language contact both with English, and with many indigenous Amerindian languages. Sometimes we find two words for the same extra-linguistic reality: for instance to designate cranberry, *atoca* comes from an Amerindian language and *canneberge* is a word of unknown origin. *Caribou* is used for a grey north American fox; *ouaouaron* for a toad; *achigan* for a black perch; also typically Canadian are the words *mocassins, anorak, kayak, parka, igloo, toboggan.* Place names are often taken from First Nations languages: for example *Quebec*, which refers to the narrowing of the St Lawrence river where the city is built: *Gaspé* which means 'extremity' and refers to the spot where Jacques Cartier put the first cross. *Tadoussac, Rimouski, Chicoutimi, Saguenay, Natashquan, Matawin, Kujjuaq, Matane, Outaouais, Oka, Abitibi,* and many other names of towns, rivers and lakes are borrowings from Amerindian languages.

Borrowings from English
Many words have been borrowed from English (*la drave*, from English *to drive* – meaning driving logs on rivers). Some of these borrowed, adapted and created words have become part of what can be classed as standard Quebec French. Others, though used by most speakers of Quebec French, tend to be reserved for informal types of settings (*binnes* instead of *fèves au lard*). Still other words such as *char* may be restricted to working-class speech in certain regions or to informal settings. Other words characteristic of Quebec French are English words which have been given a French character: flour in English becomes *fleur; bother* becomes *bâdrer; enfirouaper* comes from 'in fur wrapped'. Thibault (1980), Deshaies (1981), and Lemieux and Cedergren (1985) all provide interesting accounts of the history of English borrowings.

Pronunciation of Quebec French

*Usually what the hearer perceives as the most salient difference
between Canadian French and European French is the pronunciation.
In fact, the phonological system of Quebec French is, by and large,
very like Standard European French. It is the phonetic realisations of
the phonemes which are different and which give Canadian French its
distinctive 'flavour'. In addition, the prosodic system is also slightly
different and again this makes Canadian French 'sound' different.
Vowels[6]*

Nasals

Quebec French still has the four nasal vowels, /ɛ̃/, /œ̃/, /ɔ̃/ and /ɑ̃/, (as
in *vin, un, vont* and *vent*, respectively) which European French had
until relatively recently, but now has only three, /ɛ̃/, /ɔ̃/ and /ɑ̃/. The
vowel /œ̃/ has been lost, by and large, and /ɛ̃/ is used instead. /ɛ̃/ is
pronounced [ẽ] rather than [ɛ̃].   The nasal vowel /ɑ̃/, found, for
example, in *pendant*, /pɑ̃dɑ̃/, which is a back vowel in European
French, is often 'fronted', i.e., produced further forward in the mouth,
in Quebec, giving [pãdã]. This difference in articulation makes it
sound a little more like the vowel /ɛ̃/, as in *pin*, [pɛ̃].

/a/ and /ɑ/

Quebec French also maintains the one-time distinction between /a/
and /ɑ/, as in *patte – pâte* which has now disappeared in European
French in the speech of all except elderly or very careful speakers.
This is also the case for /ɛ/ and /ɛ:/ (*mètre – maître*). Another very
distinctive feature of Canadian vowels is that /a/ is pronounced [ɑ] or
[o] in final position, for example, *Canada* is pronounced [kanadɑ] or
[kanado].

---

6   An excellent comprehensive account of the Quebec phonological system is
     provided in Papen (1998).

/i/, /y/ and /u/

In Quebec French, the high vowels /i/, /y/ and /u/ are lax[7] in stressed closed syllables (i.e., ending with a consonant) except for the lengthening consonants /z/, /ʒ/, /v/, /r/ and the cluster /vr/. For example, /vit/ is pronounced /vɪt/.[8] This laxing of the high vowels is one of the features which gives the pronunciation of Canadian French its distinctiveness. It is common to all varieties of French in Canada. Laxing is used variably in unstressed syllables.

Diphthongisation

Another feature of Canadian pronunciation which gives it its distinctiveness is the use of diphthongs which do not exist in European French. So *mère* may be pronounced [mair].

The sequence oi

The pronunciation of the sequence *oi*, as found, for example, in *moi*, is also a very salient feature of Canadian French. In Standard Quebec French, one finds *moi, toi,* as [mwa] and [twa]. The vowel is found in lengthened form, [wa:],[9] in closed syllables, for example in *soir* [swa:r]. Older usage had [we] which was often used to stereotype Canadian French, often spelled as 'mwé', in attempts to reproduce speech patterns in the written code. This is now no longer much used and is replaced by [wa].

---

7   'Lax' is a phonetic term which, when applied to vowels, means that the vowel is generally produced with less muscular tension, is more open and shorter than a tense vowel (see Martin, 1996: 114).
8   The lax vowel in this case is similar to the English vowel in 'sit'.
9   A colon is used in phonetic transcription to indicate added length.

Consonants

/t/ and /d/

The principal feature which makes the consonants 'sound' different from European French is the affrication of the dentals /t/ and /d/ before high front vowels and glides. Affrication involves pronouncing /t/ as [ts] and /d/ as [dz], as in the following examples: *typique* [tsipik] and *dune* [dzyn]. Dentals can optionally palatalize[10] before /j/ or even delete: *canadien*, [kanadzjɛ̃] or [kanajɛ̃].

/r/

/r/ in Canadian French is undergoing change in progress. Traditionally, the older European French pronunciation was favoured (as it is still found in certain regions of France). Originally in the French of France, /r/ was an apico-dental trill or flap.[11] Now in France young urban speakers universally use a uvular fricative and even a velar fricative.[12] In Canada, a somewhat similar situation pertains. Young people use the uvular or even the velar variant and older or rural people still use the trill or flap. At times, in word-final position, when it is preceded by a long diphthongized vowel, it deletes, so *faire* is pronounced [fai]. 'r' deletion is found, as it is in popular European French, in word-final position, when preceded by a consonant: *sucre*, [syk]. There is final consonant cluster simplification which is a feature of French world-wide: /r/ and /l/ delete after obstruents (*table*, [tab]).

---

10 To 'palatalize' means to be pronounced in the region of the hard palate, i.e., further back in the mouth than would be the case for a dental articulation.

11 'Apico-dental' refers to an articulation involving the apex (tip) of the tongue coming in contact with the region of the mouth behind the upper teeth. In the case of a 'trill', there are repeated contacts between these articulating organs, in the case of a 'flap', there is one.

12 A 'fricative' is a consonant whose articulation involves a constriction of the air at some point in the vocal tract. Typical fricative consonants are: /f/, /v/, /s/, /z/, as in 'fois', 'vin', 'si' and 'zone'. The term 'velar' refers to constriction in the region of the soft palate and 'uvular' to the region of the 'uvula', an appendage at the back of the soft palate. Typically, the European French /r/ is articulated as a 'uvular fricative'.

150

/l/

The deletion of /l/ is generalised in Canadian French (Ashby, 1984; Armstrong, 1996; Howard, Lemée and Regan, 2006), and is further advanced than in European French (Beaulicu, 1995; Regan, Howard and Lemée, to appear). /l/ deletes in the definite articles and pronoun clitics *la, les, lui* and in final /l/ in *il, elle*. In Canadian French we find sequences such as *sur la table* [satab] or *elle est partie* [aparti]. Sometimes /l/ is inserted between clitic pronouns *ça* or *on* (for example, one finds *ça l'arrive souvent*).

Acadian French

Acadian French is found in New Brunswick (where it has official status), Nova Scotia, and Prince Edward Island. A comprehensive account of Acadian French is found in Beaulieu and Cichocki (2002) as well as, for instance, Dubois and Boudreau (1994), Beaulieu and Cichocki (2005), Dubé (2005), Lord (2005), Papen (1998: 172–173). There are different varieties within the overall category 'Acadian French'. Borrowing phenomena tend to behave differently in Acadian French from Quebec. For instance, where all Canadian varieties borrow verbs, only Acadian varieties borrow prepositions. Acadian is different also from Quebec French in that it tends to preserve more rural vernacular features *je...ons* or *i...ont* (which has disappeared from Quebec French), see Beaulieu and Cichocki (2005).

The sounds of Acadian French

The phonology of Acadian French is described in detail in Papen (1998: 173). Acadian French sounds are both similar to and different from those of Quebec French. The aspects which are similar tend to be those seen mainly in the more conservative and rural varieties of Quebec French. Like Quebec French, Acadian French has laxed vowels in stressed closed syllables or in unstressed syllables. Also, as in Quebec French, vowels are lengthened before lengthening consonants. Open and closed /e/ contrast in word final position: *dé – dais, pré – près* . In stressed closed syllables we find [ɛ] or [ɛ:]. Before /r/ the open mid vowels /ɛ/, /œ/ and /ɔ/ are variably closed to [e], [ø] and [o]; *mer* [me:r] *port* [po:r], as in conservative Quebec speech. Before /r/ + consonant cluster, /ɛ/ is variably realised as [æ] or [a] *couverte* [kuvart], also like Quebec, as we saw earlier. As in Quebec pronunciation, the /ɛ/–/ɛ:/ and /a/–/ɑ/ distinctions are maintained, as is the very typical word-final /a/ pronounced [ɑ], and [ɔ] as in *cas* [kɔ].

Differences between Acadian French pronunciation and Quebec pronunciation are however also numerous. The principal difference is that Acadian French has only the three nasal vowels /ɛ̃/, /ɑ̃/ and /ɔ̃/, like European French, whereas, as we saw earlier, Quebec French retains the fourth nasal vowel /œ̃/ which was formerly part of the vowel system of French in France.

Differences in the realisation of vowels
between Acadian French and Quebec French

In Acadian French, /o/ becomes /u/ or /ʊ/ in certain words for example *beaucoup* is pronounced [bʊkʊ], *chose* [ʃʊz]. Before a nasal consonant, /ɔ/ is variably /ʊ/, /o/ or /œ/. *personne* [parsʊn] [parsœn], *comment* [kʊmã] [komã].

oi is slightly differently realised than in Quebec French. In final syllables, *moi is* pronounce [mwe], for instance. *oi* in final closed syllables is variably [wɛ:] or [we:].

As regards nasal vowels, there are regional differences in their pronunciation, and there is a general tendency to a restructuring of the nasal vowel phonemic system with a clear tendency towards lower vowel variants in final word positions.

Differences in the realisation of consonants
between Acadian French and Quebec French

Consonants in the Acadian system are similar in general to those of Quebec with some differences.

/h/ is pronounced /ɦ/ haut

/t/ and /d/ before a glide /j/ are palatalized ; *tiens* [tjɛ̃] – [tʲɛ̃]

/t/ and /d/ are not affricated before high front vowels and glides as in Quebec French. Mougeon (1980); Mougeon and Beniak (1981); Mougeon (1981); Beniak, Mougeon et al. (1985); Mougeon and Beniak (1989); Chaudenson, Mougeon and Beniak (1993) and Mougeon and Beniak (1993) all note that this is one of the most important differences between the phonetics of Acadian French and Quebec French.

/k/ and /g palatalize or become pre-palatal affricates before front vowels: *guêpe* is pronounced variably [gɛ:p] – [dʒɛ:p]/

The phoneme /r/ has the following two variants: [r] and [ɾ], except in word final position where it is devoiced or deleted. In general, older speakers tend to use the two variants [r] and [ɾ] and younger speakers also have [ʀ].

Ontario French

Perhaps one of the main differences between Quebec French and Acadian French on the one hand, and Ontario French on the other, is the issue of language contact. Unlike Quebec French, Ontario French is in a permanent situation of language contact with English. There have been French speakers in Ontario since the beginning of French settlements in Canada. Where Ontario borders Quebec, they are in the majority and tend to use French at home and attrition is low here. Younger speakers use fewer anglicisms than elsewhere in Ontario. Where Francophone speakers are in a minority there is a greater tendency to use English at home. Young people use English more amongst themselves, use more anglicisms, have more restricted access to Francophone speakers with consequent language change frequently involving morphological simplification and regularisation such as levelling of *avoir* and *être* in auxiliary positions (Mougeon and Beniak, 1981 and 1991).

Variation caused by language contact: Ontario French

Ontario French derives much of its character from the fact of restriction of access to native speakers and native Canadian French. In the case of variability in many minority languages, there is often structural simplification – the result of speakers' lack of contact with native speech and so a restricted usage. Mougeon shows that these simplifications point up fragile areas in the linguistic system. He outlines a case of simplification which relates to verbal morphology, especially third person plural of the present tense (Thomas, 1989). As a result of restricted access one finds: transfer, structural simplification and stylistic reduction (these are all also features of the speech of second language speakers).

The loss of stylistic variation is the result of a considerable lessening of use of French in the home situation. This brings about a lack of contact with the vernacular which is perceptible in the speakers' usage. Stylistic reduction brings a loss of social meaning. Communication in general is not affected but there is a loss of social indicators and range of registers. Such speech is still however very much an L1 and is quite different from French learnt as a second language. Mougeon emphasises that in general the speech of Ontario adolescents is still quite different from the speech of L2 speakers except in the case of a small minority of speakers who do not maintain their use of French in the private domain of the *foyer* and have very restricted access to native speech.

Avoir/être alternation
Ontarian speakers have as features alternation of *avoir/être* (which exists in many other varieties of French). This is a general tendency to regularisation of the system of auxiliaries in French which has always existed. Those speakers who maintain a high usage of French in their

154

daily lives have a much greater usage of *avoir/ être* alternation despite this general levelling tendency. Those speakers with a low or medium level of maintenance of French have a much higher incidence of *avoir* usage in *être* contexts (this follows the direction of children and L2 speakers). Verb has an effect on the degree of usage of *avoir* as auxiliary. Conservative speakers of Ontarian French almost never use *avoir* with the verb *aller*. This is probably due to the fact that *aller* is one of the most frequently used verbs in French.

A and de alternation
Ontario speakers use alternation between the prepositions *à* and *de*. This is peculiar to Canadian French by and large, though it is used in working class speech in European French. Mougeon found that the speakers whose level of maintenance of French is low do not in fact use the possessive *à (la chaise à ma mère)* despite the fact that interviews were deliberately informal. It was however used by those who were less restricted speakers. The restricted speakers attend French schools where they hear generally less of the vernacular of the surrounding language community, and so despite certain apparent indices of vernacular usage such as *avoir/ être* alternation, they are in fact not in possession of vernacular variants. Levelling of third person plural forms is a feature particularly of those who are restricted speakers *(les vieux fait rien)*.The conservative norm of Ontarian French is close to the standard norm. Schooling through French also militates against levelling. Mougeon concludes that it is the degree of restriction which is the most important factor in the use of non-native variants or what sound like English influenced variants. Only very restricted speakers use patterns similar to L2 speakers or children.

The sounds of Ontario French

The sounds of Ontario French are very similar to those of Quebec French. There is an increasing tendency in Ontario for speakers to adopt Standard Canadian French pronunciation. There is a decreasing use of close /e/ in *mère*; the distinction between /ɛ/ and /ɛ:/ is being steadily lost; a decrease in high vowel laxing; final /a/ increasingly pronounced [a] rather than [ɔ] ([kanada] rather than [kanadɔ]); and an increasing use of uvular /ʀ/. Papen (1987) points out that bilingual speakers in Ontario are aspirating initial voiceless plosive consonants; /p/, /t/ and /k/, (which is a feature of English and which European French does not do), and that intonation patterns are beginning to sound like those of English.

West of Ontario

Here are minority French speakers whose ancestors were immigrants from Quebec. These speakers are surrounded by English speakers and for this reason are much more in danger of assimilation than other French speaking groups in Canada. They are supported by the Fédération des Francophones hors Québec. In this region, also, are the Métis who are of mixed Amerindian and French descent. Métis is a mixture of conservative Canadian French and innovations from local Indian languages, such as Cree. This mixed Cree-French called *métif* (*Michif*) has a syntax 'half French' and 'half Cree' where the noun group follows French *métis* grammar rules and the verb group follows Cree rules. Métis speakers pronounce /t/ and /d/ [tʃ] and [dʒ] rather than the Quebec [tˢ], [dᶻ]. Close mid vowels /e/, /ø/ and /o/ tend to be pronounced as high vowels [i], [y] and [u]; *été* is [iti]. This may be due to the influence of Cree.

The French spoken by anglophones

Recently, interesting studies have been made of the French spoken by English L1 speakers. A study (Sankoff, Thibault et al., 1997) of discourse markers (*bon, alors, là, tu sais)* in the speech of anglophone Montreal speakers found that the most fluent speakers used more of

156

these native discourse markers and that their use was an indication of the integration of the speakers into the speech community. Similar results were found by Nagy, Blondeau et al. (2003), who found a correlation between contact with the francophone community and native-like use of subject doubling. This is similar to results found in second language studies which examine the effects of contact with native speakers (Regan, 1995).

Conclusion

All languages are undergoing constant change, but changes in French in Canada display some particularly interesting features. Indications of language contact effects such as borrowing from English and code-switching are significant. However, it seems that such effects have been overstated at times, and that many features which have been thought to be due to contact with English are instead simply variable features which have always existed in French in Canada, whether as elements from seventeenth century France which have been retained or as features which have evolved internally within Canada over time.

In any event it is clear that language attitudes are changing from those previous to the Quiet Revolution where linguistic insecurity was widespread ('We don't speak Good French'), to a current situation where such insecurity is very much on the way to disappearing, and the evolution of the language is perhaps being affected by a desire for equality with what is in many regions the dominant language, English, and which gives rise to innovations such as the feminisation of titles or new semantic fields such as that of technological terms. Most of the changes which are taking place however are simply either those which are taking place in Romance languages in general, or are internal to Canadian French, are part of the on-going development of the vernacular speech of the community and not, in most cases, a sign of overwhelming influence of English.

Bibliography

Amireault, V., 2004, 'Les immigrants au Québec', in *Québec français*, 132, hiver 2004, pp. 58–9.

Andersen, R., 1984, 'The One-to-One Principle of interlanguage constuction', in *Language Learning*, 34, pp. 77–95.

Armstrong, N., 1996, 'Variable deletion of French /l/: linguistic, social and stylistic factors', in *Journal of French Language Studies*, 6, pp. 1–22.

Ashby, W., 1984, 'The elision of /l/ in French clitic pronouns and articles', in Pulgram, E., (ed.), *Romanitas: Studies in Romance Linguistics*, Ann Arbor: University of Michigan Press, pp. 1–16.

Auger, J. and A. Valdman, 1999, 'Letting French Students Hear the Diverse Voices of Francophony', in *The Modern Language Journal*, 83, pp. 403–12.

Barbaud, P., 1997, 'La diglossie québécoise', in Dvorak, M., (ed.), *Canada et bilinguisme*, Rennes: Presses de l'Université de Rennes, pp. 65–82.

Barthomeuf, J., 1991, 'L'observation du travail de groupe en immersion', in *Le Journal de l'IMMERSION Journal*, 15: 2, pp. 19–25.

Basque, M., 2000, 'Les Acadiens', in Plourde, M., (sous la dir. de), *Le français au Québec: 400 ans d'histoire et de vie*, Québec, Conseil de la langue française: Les Publications du Québec, Fides, pp. 22–4.

Basque, M., I. McKee-Allain, L. Cardinal, P. E. LeBlanc et J. L. Pallister, (sous la direction de), 2000, *L'Acadie au féminin: un regard multidisciplinaire sur les Acadiennes et les Cadiennes*, avec la collaboration de Stéphanie Côté, Moncton: Université de Moncton, Chaire d'études acadiennes, Collection Mouvange.

Bayley, R. and V. Regan, 2004, 'The acquisition of sociolinguistic competence: special issue', in *Journal of Sociolinguistics*, 8: 3, pp. 323–38.

Beaulieu, L., 1995, *The social function of linguistic variation: a socio-linguistic study in four rural communities of the northeastern coast of New Brunswick*, University of South Carolina.

Beaulieu, L. and W. Cichocki, 2002, 'Le concept de réseau social dans une communauté acadienne rurale', in *Revue canadienne de linguistique*, 47: 3/4, pp. 123–50.

Beaulieu, L. and W. Cichocki, 2005, 'Continuité et changement en français acadien du Nouveau-Brunswick, Canada: le cas de l'accord sujet–verbe à la 3ème personne du pluriel'. Paper presented at Colloque Association for French Language Studies, Université de Savoie, Chambéry.

Beniak, É., R. Mougeon, et al., 1985, *Contact des langues et changement linguistique: étude sociolinguistique du français parlé à Welland (Ontario)*, Québec: Centre international de recherche sur le bilinguisme.

Blanc, M., 1993, 'French in Canada', in Sanders, C., (ed.), *French Today: Language in its social context*, Cambridge: Cambridge University Press, pp. 239–56.

Blondeau, H., 2001, 'Real-time Changes in the Paradigm of Personal Pronouns in Montreal French', in *Journal of Sociolinguistics*, 5, pp. 453–74.

Blondeau, H., N. Nagy, G. Sankoff, and P. Thibault, 2002, 'La couleur locale du français L2 des Anglo-Montréalais', in *AILE. Acquisition et Interaction en Langue Etrangère,* Encrages, 17, pp. 73–100.

Bouchard, P. and R. Y. Bourhis, (eds), 2002, 'L'aménagement linguistique au Québec: 25 ans d'application de la Charte de la langue française', in *Revue d'aménagement linguistique*, automne 2002, Special Issue.

Bouchard, P., N. Guilloton, P. Vachon-L'Heureux, J.-F. De Pietro, M.-J. Béguelin, M.-J. Mathieu and M.-L. Moreau, 1999, *La féminisation des noms de métier, fonctions, grades ou titres, au Québec, en Suisse romande, en France et en Communauté française de Belgique*, Service de la Langue française, Ministère de la Commmunauté française: Éditions Duculot, Collection Français et Société 10.

Boudreau, A. and L. Dubois, (eds), 1998, 'Le français langue maternelle, dans les collèges et les universités en milieu minoritaire', Congrès annuel, Moncton, Centre de recherche en linguistique appliquée, Université de Moncton.

Boulanger, J. C., (ed.), 1993, *Dictionnaire québécois d'aujourd'hui*, Saint-Laurent, Québec: Dicorobert.

Bourhis, R. Y., 1997, 'Language Policies and Language Attitudes: Le Monde de la Francophonie', in Coupland, N., and A. Jaworski, (eds), *Sociolinguistics: A Reader and Coursebook*, London: Macmillan, pp. 306–22.

Bright, W., (ed.), 1992, *International Encyclopedia of Linguistics*, 4 vols., New York, Oxford: Oxford University Press.

Brown, C., (sous la dir. de), 1988, *Histoire générale du Canada*, Montréal: Boréal, (Édition française dirigée par P.-A. Linteau).

Brown, C., (ed.), 2002, *The Illustrated History of Canada*, Toronto: Key Porter Books.

Buckner, P., 2003, 'Introduction', in *British Journal of Canadian Studies*, 16: 1, pp. 1–6, (Special Issue on Migration from England to Canada).

Caldwell, G., 2002, 'La Charte de la langue française vue par les anglophones', in Bouchard, P. and R. Y. Bourhis, (eds), *Revue d'aménagement linguistique*, automne 2002, Special Issue, *L'aménagement linguistique au Québec: 25 ans d'application de la Charte de la langue française*.

Canada, 1867, Constitution *Act 1867*, Ottawa: Department of Justice.

Canada. Commissioner of Official Languages, 2000, *Annual Report 1999–2000*, Ottawa: Minister of Public Works and Government Services.

Canada. Commissioner of Official Languages, 2000, *Official Languages Act, 1988 Synopsis*, (www.ocol-clo.gc.ca).

Canada. Office of the Commissioner of Official Languages, 2001, *Our Official Languages: As a Century Ends and a Millennium Begins*, (www.ocol-clo.gc.ca/archives/op_ap/histo/annivers/annivers_e.htm).

Canada Commissioner of Official Languages, 2003a, 'The Royal Commission on Bilingualism and Biculturalism in the Present:

Results, Recommendations and Repercussions for the future', address delivered at McGill University, Montreal, 25 May 2003. (www.ocol-clo.gc.ca/archives/sp_al/2002/2003-05-26_e.htm).

Canada. Commissioner of Official Languages, 2003b, *Annual Report 2002–2003*, Ottawa: Minister of Public Works and Government Services.

Canada. Commissioner of Official Languages, 2003c, *The Supreme Court of Canada Clarifies the Role of the Courts in Protecting Language Rights*, (www.ocol-clo.gc.ca/archives/nr_cp/2003/ 2003-11-06_e.htm).

Canada. Commissioner of Official Languages, 2004a, *Linguistic Duality at the Heart of Our Identity: Commissioner Expects Concrete Results*, (www.ocol-clo.gc.ca/archives/nr_cp/004/ 2004-02-02.e.htm).

Canada. Commissioner of Official Languages, 2004b, *Walking the Talk: Language of Work in the Federal Public Service*, (www.ocol-clo.gc.ca/archives/sst_es/2004/work_travail_2004_ e.htm).

Canada. Commissioner of Official Languages, 2005a, *Annual Report 2004–2005,* vol. 1, Ottawa: Minister of Public Works and Government Services.

Canada. Commissioner of Official Languages, 2005b, *Annual Report 2004–2005,* vol. 2, Ottawa: Minister of Public Works and Government Services.

Canada. Commissioner of Official Languages, 2006, *Annual Report 2005–2006*, Ottawa: Minister of Public Works and Government Services.

Canada. Department of Justice, 1982, *The Canadian Charter of Rights and Freedoms*, (www.canada.justice.gc.ca/loire/charte/const_ en.html).

Canada. Department of Justice, 1988, *Official Languages Act.*

Canada. Department of Justice, 1992, *Official Languages (Communications with and Services to the Public) Regulations.*

Canada. Privy Council Office, 2003, *The Next Act: New Momentum for Canada's Linguistic Duality: The Action Plan for Official Languages*, (www.pco-bcp.gc.ca).

Canada. Standing Joint Committee on Official Languages, 1997, *3rd Report of the Standing Joint Committee on Official Languages*, (www.parl.gc.ca/committees352/olan/reports/03_199704/toce. html).

Canada. Statistics Canada, 2002, *Profile of languages in Canada: English, French and many others*, Ottawa, catalogue no. 96F0039XIE2001005.

Canada. Statistics Canada, 2003, *Use of English and French at work*, Ottawa, catalogue no. 96F0030XIE2001011.

Canada. Statistics Canada, 2004, *2001 Census Dictionary*, 92–378–XIE, (www.statcan.ca/english/census01/Products/Reference/dict/index.html).

Canada. Travaux publics et Services gouvernementaux, 1996, *Le Guide du rédacteur*.

Cardinal, L., 2003, *Difficult Citizenship: Pierre Elliott Trudeau and the Politics of Recognition in Canada*, Inaugural Lecture, University College Dublin: Faculty of Arts.

Cardinal, L., 2004, 'Citizenship Politics in Canada and the Legacy of Pierre Elliott Trudeau', in Boyer, P., L. Cardinal and D. Headon, (eds), *From Subjects to Citizens: A Hundred Years of Citizenship in Australia and Canada*, Ottawa: University of Ottawa Press, pp. 163–78.

Carlson, L., 1992, 'Observing Communication and Interaction Patterns in French Immersion Classrooms: Implications for consultation.' Unpublished Master of Arts, University of Toronto.

Castonguay, C., 1994, *L'assimilation linguistique: mesure et evolution, 1971–1986*, Québec: Les Publications du Québec.

Chambers, G., 2000, 'Les relations entre Anglophones et francophones', in Plourde, M., (sous la dir. de), *Le français au Québec: 400 ans d'histoire et de vie*, Québec, Conseil de la langue française: Les Publications du Québec, Fides, pp. 319–25.

Chaudenson, R., R. Mougeon, et al., 1993, *Vers une approche panlectale de la variation du français*, Didier: Didier Érudition.

Chaudron, C., 1986, 'Teachers' Priorities in Correcting French Learners' Errors in French Immersion Class', in Day, R. R. (ed.), *Talking to Learn – Conversations in Second Language Acquisition*, Rowley, MA: Newbury House Publishers.

Chevrier, M., 1997, 'The Rationale for Québec's Language Policy', *Espoir*, September. (www.mri.gouv.qc.ca/la_bibliotheque/langue/loi-langue_ syn_an.html).

Cholette, G., 1993, *L'Office de la langue française de 1961 à 1974: Regard et témoignage*, Quebec: Institut québécois de recherche sur la culture, Office de la langue française.

Churchill, S., 1998, *Official Languages in Canada: Changing the Language Landscape*, Canada: Canadian Heritage, New Canadian Perspectives Series.

Cleghorn, A. and F. Genesee, 1984, 'Languages in conflict: An ethnographic study of interaction in an immersion school', in *TESOL Quarterly*, 18: 4, pp. 595–625.

Confederation–Confédération, 1967, Toronto: R.G. McLean.

Conrick, M., 1998, 'Linguistic Perspectives on the Feminisation of Professional Titles in Canadian French', in *British Journal of Canadian Studies*, 13: 1, pp. 164–80.

Conrick, M., 2002a, 'Language Policy and Gender Issues in Contemporary French', in Salhi, K., (ed.), *French in and out of France: Language Policies, Intercultural Antagonisms and Dialogue*, Oxford, Bern, Frankfurt am Main, New York, Wien: Peter Lang, pp. 205–35.

Conrick, M., 2002b, 'French in the Americas', in Salhi, K., (ed.), *French in and out of France: Language Policies, Intercultural Antagonisms and Dialogue*, Oxford, Bern, Frankfurt am Main, New York, Wien: Peter Lang, pp. 237–63.

Conrick, M., 2005a, 'Language Choice and Education Rights in Quebec: Bill 101 passes the Supreme Court test?', in *French Studies Bulletin*, no. 97, winter, pp. 9–13.

Conrick, M., 2005b, 'La modernisation du français en Acadie: les médias et la représentation linguistique et professionnelle des femmes', in Clermont, G. and J. Gallant, (eds), *La modernité en Acadie,* Moncton, New Brunswick: Chaire d'Études acadiennes, Université de Moncton, pp. 75–99.

Conrick, M., 2006, 'Canadian Language Policy in an International Context: the Impact of Official Languages Legislation in Canada and Ireland', in Anctil, Pierre and Z. Bernd, (eds), *Canada from the outside in: New Trends in Canadian Studies / Le Canada vu d'ailleurs: tendances nouvelles en études canadiennes*, Bruxelles, Bern, Berlin, Frankfurt am Main New York, Oxford, Wien: Peter Lang, *Canadian Studies*, vol. 7, editor Serge Jaumain, pp. 217–32.

Cook, R., 2002, 'The Triumph and Trials of Materialism (1900–1945)', in Brown, Craig, (ed.), *The Illustrated History of Canada*, Toronto: Key Porter Books, pp. 377–472.

Côté, R., (sous la dir. de) 2001, *Québec 2002: Annuaire politique, social, économique et culturel*, Québec: Éditions Fides.

Coveney, A., 2000, 'Vestiges of *nous* and the 1st person plural verb in informal spoken French', in *Language Sciences*, 22, pp. 447–81.

Cummins, J. and M. Swain, 1986, *Bilingualism in Education*, London: Longman.

Day, E. and S. Shapson, 1988, 'Provincial Assessment of Early and Late French Immersion Programs in British Columbia, Canada'. Paper presented at the Annual Meeting of the American Educational Research Association, New Orleans Publisher ERIC Document Reproduction Service No ED 295 964.

Day, E. and S. Shapson, 1996, *Studies in Immersion Education*, Clevedon: Multilingual Matters.

de Courcy, M., 2002, *Learners' Experiences of Immersion Education: Case Studies of French and Chinese*, Clevedon: Multilingual Matters.

Deshaies, D., 1981, *Le français parlé dans la ville de Québec: une étude sociolinguistique*, Québec: CIRB, G–I.

Dewaele, J.-M. and V. Regan, 2001, 'The use of colloquial words in advanced French interlanguage', in Foster-Cohen, S. and A. Nizegorodcew, (eds), *EUROSLA Yearbook 1*, Amsterdam and Philadelphia: John Benjamins, pp. 51–67.

Dickinson, J. and B. Young, 2003, *A Short History of Quebec*, Montreal and Kingston: McGill–Queen's University Press (3rd edition).

Dorian, N., 1981, *Language Death. The Life Cycle of a Scottish Gaelic Dialect*, Philadelphia: University of Pennsylvania Press.

Dostie, G., 2005, 'Variation et régularité sémantique. Réflexions à partir du marqueur 'fait que' en français québécois'. Paper presented at Colloque Association of French Language Studies, Université de Savoie, Chambéry.

Druon, M., H. d'Encausse et H. Biancotti, 'Lettre ouverte à Jacques Chirac', *Le Figaro*, le 9 janvier 1998.

Dubé, P., 2005, 'Francophonies D'Amerique', in *Francophonies d'Amérique*, 19, pp. 9–16.

Dubé, P., and M.-L. Lord, 2005, 'Francophonies D'Amerique', in *Francophonies d'Amérique*, 19 (special issue).

Dubois, L. and A. Boudreau, 1994, *Les Acadiens et leur(s) langue(s): quand le français est minoritaire*, Moncton: Centre de recherche en linguistique appliquée de l'Université de Moncton.

Durham, Earl of (John George Lambton), 1902 [1839], *The Report of the Earl of Durham, Her Majesty's High Commissioner and Governor-General of British North America,* London: Methuen.

Durham, J. G. L., 1990 [1839], *Le Rapport Durham*, Montréal: l'Hexagone. (Traduction et introduction de Denis Bertrand et d'Albert Desbiens)

Flikeid, K., 1989, 'Recherches sociolinguistiques sur les parlers acadiens du Nouveau-Brunswick et de la Nouvelle-Écosse', in Mougeon, R. and É. Beniak, (eds), *Le Français canadien parlé hors Québec: Aperçu sociolinguistique,* Quebec: Les Presses de l'Université Laval, pp. 183–99.

Fox, P., 1999, 'Royal Commissions', in *The Canadian Encyclopedia*, Toronto: McClelland and Stewart, p. 2045.

Freed, B., N. Segalowitz, et al., 2004, 'Context of learning and second language fluency in French: Comparing Regular Classroom, Study Abroad, and Intensive Domestic Immersion Programs', in *Studies in Second Language Acquisition, Special Issue: Learning Context and its Effects on Second Language Acquisition*, Collentine, J. and Freed, B. (Guest eds), 26: 2, pp. 275–301.

Frenette, Y., 1998, *Brève Histoire des Canadiens français*, Montreal: Boréal.

Froc, M., 1995, 'Error correction in French immersion', in *Canadian Modern Language Review*, 51: 4, pp. 708–17.

Gendron, J.-D., 1973, *Report of the Commission of Inquiry on the position of the French language and on language rights in Quebec,* Quebec: Government of Quebec.

Genesee, F., 1983, 'Bilingual education of majority language children: The immersion experiments in review', in *Applied Psycholinguistics*, 4, pp. 1–46.

Genesee, F., 1987, *Learning through two languages: Studies of immersion and bilingual education,* Rowley, MA: Newbury House.

Genesee, F., N. Holobow, et al., 1985, 'The linguistic and academic development of English speaking children in French schools: Grade four outcomes', in *Canadian Modern Language Review*, 41: 4, pp. 669–85.

Genesee, F. and W. E. Lambert, 1983, 'Trilingual education for majority language children', in *Child Development*, 54, pp. 105–14.

Gervais, D., 2003, 'Le Français au Québec', in Argod-Dutard, F., (ed.), *Quelles perspectives pour la langue française?*, Rennes, Les Lyriades: Presses Universitaires de Rennes, pp. 219–28.

Goddard, I., 1992, 'Algonkian Languages', in Bright, William, (ed.), *International Encyclopedia of Linguistics*, vol. 1, New York, Oxford: Oxford University Press, pp. 44–8.

Grosjean, F., 1982, *Life with Two Languages: An Introduction to Bilingualism,* Cambridge, MA: Harvard University Press.

Guy, G., 1995, 'Form and Function in Linguistic Variation', in Guy, G., C. Feagin, D. Schiffrin, and J. Baugh, (eds), *Towards a Social Science of Language. Papers in Honor of William Labov*, Volume 1, Amsterdam and Philadelphia: John Benjamins, pp. 221–52.

Harley, B., 1993, 'Instructional strategies and SLA in early French immersion', in *Studies in Second Language Acquisition*, 15, pp. 245–59.

Harley, B., 1994, 'Maintaining French as a second language in adulthood', in *Canadian Modern Language Review*, 50: 4, pp. 688–713.

Harvey, F., 2000, 'Le français menacé', in Plourde, Michel, (sous la dir. de), *Le français au Québec: 400 ans d'histoire et de vie*, Québec, Conseil de la langue française: Les Publications du Québec, Fides, pp. 139–53.

Heller, M., 1998, *Quelle norme enseigner en milieu minoritaire. Le français langue maternelle dans les collèges et les universités en milieu minoritaire*, Moncton: Éditions d'Acadie.

Henripin, J., 2005, 'Denatality, Aging and Immigration: the challenges of changing demographics', in *Policy Options*, March–April, pp. 61–5.

Hickey, T., 1998, 'Early immersion in Ireland: The Naionra experience', in Regan, V., (ed.), *Contemporary approaches to second language acquisition in social context*, Dublin: University College Dublin Press, pp. 46–62.

Houle, F., 2004, 'Canadian Citizenship and Multiculturalism', in Boyer, P., L. Cardinal and D. Headon, (eds), *From Subjects to Citizens: A Hundred Years of Citizenship in Australia and Canada*, Ottawa: University of Ottawa Press, pp. 217–28.

Howard, M., I. Lemée, et al., 2006, 'The L2 acquisition of a phonological variable: the case of /l/ deletion in French', in *Journal of French Language Studies*, 16, pp. 1–24.

Institute for Research on Public Policy, (ed.), 1999, *As I recall / Si je me souviens bien: Historical Perspectives / Perspectives historiques*, Montreal: Institute for Research on Public Policy, with John Meisel, Guy Rocher and Arthur Silver.

Ireland, 2003, *Acht na dTeangacha Oifigiúla 2003 /Official Languages Act 2003*.

Johnson, R. K. and M. Swain, (eds), 1997, *Immersion education: International perspectives*, Cambridge: Cambridge University Press.

King, R., 1994, 'Subject–Verb Agreement in Newfoundland French', in *Language Variation and Change*, 6, pp. 239–53.

King, R., and T. Nadasdi, 1999, 'The Expression of Evidentiality in French–English Bilingual Discourse', *Language and Society*, 28, pp. 355–66.

Kowal, M. and M. Swain, 1997, 'From semantic to syntactic processing: How can we promote metalinguistic awareness in the French immersion classroom?', in Johnson, R. K. and M. Swain, (eds), 1997, *Immersion Education: International perspectives*, Cambridge: Cambridge University Press, pp. 284–309.

Krashen, S. D., 1984, 'Immersion: Why it works and what it has taught us', in *Language and Society*, 12, pp. 61–4.

Krashen, S. D., 1985, *The Input Hypothesis*, London and New York: Longman.

Labov, W., 1994, *Principles of Linguistic Change: internal factors*, Oxford: Blackwell.

Labov, W., 2001, *Principles of Linguistic Change: social factors*, Oxford: Blackwell.

Lacoursière, J., 1997, *Histoire populaire du Québec*, Sillery, Quebec: Septentrion, vol. 4.

Laing, G., 1999, 'Bilingualism and Biculturalism, Royal Commission on', in *The Canadian Encyclopedia*, Toronto: McClelland and Stewart, p. 235.

Lalonde, M., 1974, *Speak White*, Paris: L'Hexagone.

Lalonde, M., 1979, *Défense et illustration de la langue québécoise*, Paris: Seghers.

Lambert, W. E. and G. R. Tucker, 1972, *Bilingual education of children*, Rowley MA: Newbury House.

Lapkin, S., (ed.), 1998, *French Second Language Education in Canada: Empirical Studies*, Toronto and Buffalo: University of Toronto Press.

Lapkin, S., D. Hart et al., 1995, 'A Canadian Interprovincial Exchange: Evaluating the Linguistic Impact of a Three-Month Stay in Quebec', in Freed B., (ed.), *Second Language Acquisition in a Study Abroad Context*, Amsterdam and Philadelphia: John Benjamins, pp. 67–94.

Lapkin, S., M. Swain et al., 1990, 'French immersion research agenda for the 1990s', in *Canadian Modern Language Review*, 46: 4, pp. 638–75.

Landry, N. and N. Lang, 2001, *Histoire de l'Acadie*, Sillery, Québec: Septentrion.

Lapierre, A., 1997, 'Le Québec et ses minorités: Quelques observations d'après les journaux et dictionnaires des 18ème et 19ème siècles', Le Colloque de Trèves en l'honneur de Hans-Joseph Niederehe, Tübingen: Max Niemeyer Verlag.

Larose, G., 2001, 'Culture plurielle et langue citoyenne', in *Bulletin du Conseil de la langue française*, 17: 3, novembre 2001, pp. 1–2.

Léard, J.-M., 1995, *Grammaire québécoise d'aujourd'hui*, Montréal: Guérin Universitaire.

LeBlanc, C., 2002, 'The conditioning of the French conditional redux: A real-time analysis', paper presented at NWAV 31, Ann Arbor (Michigan).

Lemieux, M. and H. Cedergren, 1985, *Les tendances dynamiques du français parlé à Montréal*, Québec: Office de la langue française.

Lépine, P., 1994, *Cartes anciennes, cartes originales ou reproduites*, Montréal: Bibliothèque nationale du Québec.

Leroux, M., 2003, 'Le passé recomposé: Analyse diachronique et multivariée de la valeur temporelle du passé en français oral de Hull (Québec)', Unpublished Masters Thesis, University of Ottawa, Department of Linguistics.

Leroux, M., 2004, 'Relics of the Canadian French 'past'', paper presented at NWAV 33, Ann Arbor (Michigan).

Lockerbie, I., I. Molinaro, et al., 2005, *French as the Common Language in Québec: History, Debates and Positions*, Montreal: Les Éditions Nota Bene.

Long, M., 1983, 'Does instruction make a difference?', in *TESOL Quarterly*, 17, pp. 359–82.

Long, M., 1996, 'The role of the linguistic environment in second language acquisition', in Ritchie W. C. and T. K. Bhatia, (eds), *Handbook of Language Acquisition*, New York: New York Academic Press, pp. 413–68.

Long, M., 2000, 'Focus on form in task-based language teaching', in S. Lambert and E. Shohamy, *Language policy and pedagogy*, Amsterdam and Philadelphia: John Benjamins, pp. 179–92.

Longfellow, H. W., 1886, *Evangeline*, London: Routledge.

Loranger, F., 1970, *Medium Saignant*, Ottawa: Leméac, Collection Théâtre Canadien.

Lord, M. L., 2005, 'Francophonies D'Amerique', in *Francophonies d'Amérique*, 19, pp. 17–18.

Lyster, R., 1992, 'Sociolinguistic Competence: Learning Formal and Informal French in the French Immersion Classroom', in *Modern*

Language Centre Colloquium OISE, Toronto, University of Toronto.

Lyster, R., 1994, 'The effect of functional-analytic teaching on aspects of French immersion students' sociolinguistic competence', in *Applied Linguistics*, 15, pp. 263–87.

MacLennan, H., 2005 [1945], *Two Solitudes*, Montreal and Kingston: McGill–Queen's University Press.

Maillet, A., 1979, *Pélagie-la-Charrette*, Paris: Grasset.

Martin, P., 1996, *Éléments de phonétique avec application au français*, Sainte-Foy, Quebec: Les Presses de l'Université Laval.

McLynn, F., 2005, *1759: The Year Britain Became Master of the World*, London: Atlantic Monthly Press.

McRoberts, K., 1999, *Quebec: Social Change and Political Crisis*, Toronto: Oxford University Press.

Milroy, L. and P. Muysken, (eds), 1995, *One speaker, two languages: Cross-disciplinary perspectives on code-switching*, Cambridge: Cambridge University Press.

Monnier, D., 1993, *Les choix linguistiques des travailleurs immigrants et allophones: Rapport d'une enquête réalisée en 1991*, Québec: Les Publications du Québec.

Moore, C., 2002, 'Colonization and Conflict: New France and its Rivals (1600–1760)', in Brown, Craig, (ed.), *The Illustrated History of Canada*, Toronto: Key Porter Books, pp. 95–180.

Mougeon, F., 2006, 'From grade school to university: the sociolinguistic competence in spoken French of undergraduate university students', paper presented at *Sociolinguistics Symposium 16*, Limerick, Ireland.

Mougeon, R., 1980, *Emploi et maîtrise du français parlé par les élèves des écoles de langue française dans les communautés franco-ontariennes minoritaires*, Toronto: Ministère de l'éducation, Ministère des collèges et universités.

Mougeon, R., 1981, *Le français et l'anglais écrit des élèves franco-ontariens: analyse des erreurs contenues dans un échantillon de rédactions écrites par des élèves de 12ème et 13ème années*, Toronto: Ministère de l'éducation, Ministère des collèges et universités.

Mougeon, R., 2000, 'Le français s'impose en Nouvelle-France', in Plourde, Michel, (sous la dir. de), *Le français au Québec: 400 ans d'histoire et de vie*, Québec, Conseil de la langue française: Les Publications du Québec, Fides, pp. 33–8.

Mougeon, R. and É. Beniak, 1981, 'Levelling of the 3sg/pl verb distinctions in Ontarion French', in Lantolf, J. P. and G. B. Stone, (eds), *Current research in Romance languages*, Bloomington: Indiana University Linguistics Club, pp. 126–44.

Mougeon, R. and É. Beniak, (eds), 1989, *Le français parlé hors Québec: aperçu sociolinguistique,* Quebec: Les Presses de l'Université Laval.

Mougeon, R. and É. Beniak, 1991, *Linguistic consequences of language contact and restriction: The case of French in Ontario, Canada*, Oxford: Oxford University Press.

Mougeon, R. and É. Beniak, 1993, 'Bilingualism, language shift, and institutional support for French: the case of the Franco-Ontarians', in *International Journal of the Sociology of Language*, 105–106, pp. 99–126.

Mougeon, R. and É. Beniak, 2002, *Linguistic Consequences of Language Contact and Restriction: The Case of French in Ontario, Canada*, Oxford: Clarendon Press.

Mougeon, R., C. Brent-Palmer, et al., 1982, *Le français en situation minoritaire: fréquence d'emploi et maîtrise du français parlé par les élèves des écoles de langue française dans des communautés franco-ontariennes*, Quebec: International Centre for Research on Bilingualism.

Mougeon, R., T. Nadasdi, et al., 2001, A *sociolinguistic analysis of phonetic variation in the spoken French of immersion students*, Canadian Association of Applied Linguistics, Quebec, Canada.

Mougeon, R., T. Nadasdi, et al., 2002, 'Etat de la recherche sur l'appropriation de la variation par les apprenants avancés du FL2 ou FLE', in *AILE: Acquisition et Interaction en Langue Etrangère*, 17, pp. 7–50.

Mougeon, R. and K. Rehner, 1998, *Recherches sociolinguistiques sur la variation du français parlé des élèves d'immersion*, Université York: GRALEF, Collège Glendon.

Mougeon, R. and K. Rehner, 2001, 'Variation in the spoken French of Ontario French immersion students: the case of juste vs. seulement vs. rien que', in *Modern Language Journal*, 85, pp. 398–415.

Mougeon, R., K. Rehner, et al., 2004, 'The learning of spoken French variation by immersion students from Toronto, Canada', in *Journal of Sociolinguistics*, 8: 3, pp. 408–33.

Myers-Scotton, C., 1993, *Duelling languages: grammatical structure in code-switching*, Oxford: Clarendon Press.

Nadasdi, T., R. Mougeon, et al., 2003, 'Emploi du 'futur' dans le français parlé des élèves d'immersion française', in *Journal of French Language Studies*, 13, pp. 195–219.

Nagy, N., H. Blondeau, et al., 2003, 'Second language acquisition and 'real' French: an investigation of subject doubling in the French of Montreal Anglophones', in *Language Variation and Change*, 15, pp. 73–103.

Niedzwiecki, P., 2002, *Le Langage au féminin*, Bruxelles / Paris: Labor / Castells.

Noël, D., 2000, 'Une langue qui ne capitule pas (la justice et les tribunaux)', in Plourde, Michel, (sous la dir. de), *Le français au Québec: 400 ans d'histoire et de vie*, Québec, Conseil de la langue française: Les Publications du Québec, Fides, pp. 72–9.

Oliver, M., 2001, 'Reflections on the B&B Commission', in *Isuma*, 2: 2, Summer, pp. 120–4.

Olson, C. P., 1983, 'Inequality remade: The theory of correspondence and the context of French immersion in northern Ontario', in *Journal of Education*, 165: 1, pp. 75–98.

Papen, R., 1987, 'Le métif: Le nec plus ultra des grammaires en contact', in *Revue Québécoise de Linguistique Théorique et Appliquée*, 6, pp. 57–70.

Papen, R., 1998, 'French: Canadian varieties', in Edwards, J., (ed.), *Language in Canada*, Cambridge: Cambridge University Press, pp. 160–76.

Paquette, G., 2006, 'Communiqué, Montréal le 19 juin 2006', (available at www.oqlf.gouv.ca).

Paquin, S., n.d., *The Myth of the Compact Theory of Canadian Federation*, (www.canadahistory.com/sections/papers/paperspaquin.htm).

Pawley, C., 1986, *What is the French Proficiency of Immersion Students Really Like?*, Ottawa: Ottawa Board of Education (Ontarion) Research Centre. ERIC Document Reproduction Service N. ED282 405.

Pelletier-Baillargeon, H., 2000, 'Le discours nationaliste (1850 à 1920)', in Plourde, M., (sous la dir. de), *Le français au Québec: 400 ans d'histoire et de vie*, Québec, Conseil de la langue française: Les Publications du Québec, Fides, pp. 187–90.

Pica, T., 1988, 'Interlanguage adjustments as an outcome of NS–NNS negotiated interaction', in *Language Learning*, 38, pp. 45–73.

Pica, T. and C. Doughty, 1985, 'Input and interaction in the communicative language classroom: a comparison of teacher-fronted and group activities', in Gass, S. and C. Madden, (eds), *Input in Second Language Acquisition*, Rowley, MA: Newbury House, pp. 115–32.

Picard, M., 1992, 'Aspects synchroniques et diachroniques du tu interrogatif en québécois', in *Revue Québécoise de Linguistique*, 21: 2, pp. 65–74.

Plourde, M., (sous la dir. de), 2000, *Le français au Québec: 400 ans d'histoire et de vie*, Québec, Conseil de la langue française: Les Publications du Québec, Fides.

Poplack, S., 1980, 'Sometimes I'll start a sentence in Spanish Y TERMINO EN ESPAGNOL: Towards a typology of code-switching' *Linguistics*, 18: 7/8, pp. 581–618.

Poplack, S., 1988, 'Contrasting patterns of code-switching in two communities', in Trudgill, P. and J. Cheshire, (eds), *The Sociolinguistics Reader*, London: Arnold, pp. 44–65.

Poplack, S., 1989, 'The care and handling of a megacorpus: the Ottawa–Hull French Project', in Fasold, R. and D. Schiffrin, (eds), *Language Change and Variation*, Amsterdam: Benjamins, pp. 411–45.

Poplack, S., 1990, 'Prescription, intuition et usage: le subjonctif français et la variabilité inhérente', in *Langage et Société*, 54, pp. 5–33.

Poplack, S., 1997, 'The Sociolinguistic Dynamics of Apparent Convergence', in Guy, G., C. Feagin, D. Schiffrin and J. Baugh, (eds), *Towards a Social Science of Language*, Amsterdam: John Benjamins, pp. 285–307.

Poplack, S., 1998, 'Code-switching in two communities', in Trudgill, P. and J. Cheshire, (eds), *The Sociolinguistics Reader*, London: Arnold, pp. 44–65.

Poplack, S., 2001, 'Variability, frequency, and productivity in the irrealis domain of French', in Bybee, J. and P. Hopper, (eds), *Frequency and the Emergence of Linguistic Structure*, Amsterdam: John Benjamins, pp. 405–28.

Poplack, S. and N. Dion, 2004, The French 'future' in grammar, thought and speech, paper presented at NWAV 33, Ann Arbor (Michigan).

Poplack, S. and M. Meechan, 1998, 'Introduction. How languages fit together in codemixing', in *Journal of Bilingualism*, 2: 2, pp. 127–38.

Poplack, S., D. Sankoff and C. Miller, 1988, 'The social and linguistic processes of Lexical Borrowing and Assimilation, in *Linguistics*, 26, pp. 47–104.

Poplack, S. and A. St-Amand, 2002, 'Les Récits du français québécois d'autrefois', Ottawa: Université d'Ottawa.

Poplack S. and S. Tagliamonte, 2001, *African American English in the Diaspora*, Oxford: Blackwell.

Poplack, S. and D. Turpin, 1999, 'Does the FUTUR have a future in (Canadian) French?', in *Probus*, 11, pp. 133–64.

Quebec, 2003, *Charte de la langue française*, Québec: Éditeur officiel du Québec.

Quebec. Commission des États généraux sur la situation et l'avenir de la langue française au Québec, 2001, *Le français, une langue pour tout le monde. Une nouvelle approche stratégique et citoyenne*, Québec: Commission des États généraux sur la situation et l'avenir de la langue française au Québec.

Quebec. Commission de Toponymie, 1996, *Noms et Lieux du Québec: dictionnaire illustré*, Québec: Les Publications du Québec.

Quebec. Conseil de la langue française, 2004, *Bulletin*, 20:1, May.

Quebec. Office de la langue française. Biron, Monique, 1991, *Au féminin: guide de féminisation des titres de fonction et de textes*, Québec: Les Publications du Québec.

Quebec. Office de la langue française, 2001, *Le grand dictionnaire terminologique*, (www.olf.gouv.ca/ressources/gdt_bdl.html).

Quebec. Office de la langue française, 2005, *Le français au bureau*, Montreal: Office de la langue française (6th edition).

Ray, A., 2002, 'When two worlds meet', in Brown, Craig, (ed.), *The Illustrated History of Canada*, Toronto: Key Porter Books, pp. 1–94. (Revised edition, first edition 1987).

Rebuffot, J., 1998, 'Aspects récents de l'immersion du français au Canada: Vers le renouvellement de la pédagogie immersive', in Arnau, J. and J. Artigal, (eds), *Immersion programmes: A European perspective*, Barcelona: Publicaciones de la Universidad de Barcelona, pp. 685–92.

Rebuffot, J. and R. Lyster, 1996, 'L'immersion au Canada: contextes, effets et pédagogie', in Erfurt, J., (ed.), *De la polyphonie à la symphonie: Méthodes, théories et faits de la recherche pluridisciplinaire sur le français au Canada*, Leipzig: Leipziger Universitatsverlag GmbH, pp. 277–94.

Regan, V., 1995, 'The Acquisition of Sociolinguistic Native Speech Norms: Effects of a Year Abroad on Second Language Learners of French', in Freed, B., (ed.), *Second language acquisition in a study abroad context*, Amsterdam and Philadelphia: John Benjamins, pp. 245–67.

Regan, V., 1996, 'Variation in French Interlanguage: A Longitudinal Study of Sociolinguistic Competence', in Bayley, R. and D. Preston, (eds), *Second Language Acquisition and Linguistic Variation*, Amsterdam and Philadelphia: John Benjamins, pp. 177–203.

Regan, V., 1997, 'Les apprenants avancés, la lexicalisation et l'acquisition de la compétence sociolinguistique: une approche variationniste', in *AILE: Acquisition et Interaction en Langue Etrangère*, 9, pp. 193–210.

Regan, V., 1998, 'Sociolinguistics and language learning in a study abroad context', in *Frontiers: the Interdisciplinary Journal of Study Abroad*, 4, pp. 61–91.

Regan, V., M. Howard, et al. (to appear). *The Acquisition of Socio-linguistic Competence in a Study Abroad Context*, Clevedon: Multilingual Matters.

René, N., 2001, Implantation terminologique: le role de l'Office de la langue française en matière de diffusion terminologique, Conférence présentée à Vitoria, le 13 février 2001, (available at www.oqlf.gov.qc.ca).

Rehner, K. and R. Mougeon, 1999, 'Variation in the spoken French of immersion students: to *ne* or not to *ne*, that is the sociolinguistic question', in *Canadian Modern Language Review*, 56, pp. 124–54.

Rehner, K., R. Mougeon, et al., 2003, 'The learning of sociolinguistic variation by advanced FSL learners: the case of *nous* versus *on* in immersion French', in *Studies in Second Language Acquisition*, 25, pp. 127–56.

Richards, J. C., J. Platt and H. Platt, 1992, *Longman Dictionary of Applied Linguistics*, London: Longman.

Rocher, G., 2002, 'Les dilemmes identitaires à l'origine de l'engendrement de la Charte de la langue française', in Bouchard, Pierre and Richard Y. Bourhis, (eds), *Revue d'aménagement linguistique*, automne 2002, Special Issue, *L'aménagement linguistique au Québec: 25 ans d'application de la Charte de la langue française*.

Rood, D. S., 1992, 'North American Languages', in Bright, William, (ed.), *International Encyclopedia of Linguistics, Volume 3*, New York, Oxford: Oxford University Press, pp. 110–5.

Royal Commission on Bilingualism and Biculturalism, 1965, *Preliminary Report of the Royal Commission on Bilingualism and Biculturalism*, Ottawa: Queen's Printer.

Royal Commission on Bilingualism and Biculturalism, 1967, *Report of the Royal Commission on Bilingualism and Biculturalism. Book 1, The Official Languages*, Ottawa: Queen's Printer.

Royal Commission on Bilingualism and Biculturalism, 1970, *Report of the Royal Commission on Bilingualism and Biculturalism*, Ottawa: Queen's Printer.

Sankoff, G., 2002, 'Linguistic Outcomes of Language Contact', in Chambers, J. K., P. Trudgill and N. Schilling-Estes, (eds), *The*

Handbook of Language Variation and Change, Oxford, Blackwell, pp. 638–69.

Sankoff, G. and H. Cedergren, 1973, 'Some results of a sociolinguistic study of Montreal French', in Darnell, R. (ed.), *Linguistic Diversity in Canadian Society*, Edmonton: Linguistic Research, pp. 61–88.

Sankoff, G. and H. Cedergren, 1976, *Les contraintes linguistiques et sociales de l'élision de /l/ chez les Montréalais*, Actes du 13ème Congrès international de linguistique et philologie romanes, Québec: Les Presses de l'Université Laval.

Sankoff, D. and W. Labov, 1979, 'On the uses of variable rules', *Language in Society*, 8, pp. 89–222.

Sankoff, G., P. Thibault, et al., 1997, 'Variation in the use of discourse markers in a language contact situation', in *Language Variation and Change*, 9, pp. 191–217.

Sankoff, G. and D. Vincent, 1977, 'The productive use of ne in spoken Montreal French', in Sankoff G., (ed.), *The Social Life of Language*, Philadelphia: University of Philadelphia Press, pp. 295–310.

Santerrc, L., 1990, 'Essai de définition du joual: aspect du français parlé au Québec', in Corbett, N., (ed.), *Langue et identité; le français et les francophones d'Amérique du Nord*, Québec: Les Presses de l'Université Laval, pp. 263–70.

Saywell, J., 1994, *Canada: Pathways to the Present*, Toronto: Stoddart.

Silva-Corvalan, C., 1986, 'Bilingualism and Language Change: The Extension of estar in Los Angeles Spanish', in *Language*, 62: 3, pp. 587–608.

Stennett, R. G. and L. M. Earl, 1983, *Elementary Late French Immersion Program: Preliminary Study*, London, Ontario: London Board of Education, Educational Research Services.

Swain, M., 1985, 'Communicative competence: Some roles of comprehensible input and comprehensible output in its development', in Gass, S. and C. Madden, (eds), *Input in Second Language Acquisition*, Rowley, MA: Newbury House, pp. 235–53.

Swain, M., 2000, 'French Immersion Research in Canada: Recent Contributions to SLA and Applied Linguistics', in *Annual Review of Applied Linguistics*, 20, pp. 199–212.

Swain, M., 2005, 'Immersion education: Some issues arising from the Canadian experience', paper presented at *Language in Society: Canada / Ireland*, Dublin: Canadian Embassy, Association of Canadian Studies in Ireland conference.

Swain, M. and S. Lapkin, 1989, 'Canadian immersion and adult second language learning: what's the connection?', in *Modern Language Journal*, 73: 2, pp. 150–9.

Swain, M. and S. Lapkin, 1990, 'Aspects of the sociolinguistic performance of early and later French immersion students', in Sarcella, R. C., E. S. Anderson and S. D. Krashen, (eds), *Developing communicative competence in a second language*, New York: Newbury House, pp. 41–54.

Swann, J., A. Deumert, et al., 2004, *A Dictionary of Sociolinguistics*, Edinburgh: Edinburgh University Press.

Tardif, C. and S. Weber, 1987, *The young child's experience of French immersion schooling*, Annual Meeting of the American Educational Research Association, Washington DC. ERIC Document Reproduction Service No ED 281 395.

Termote, M., 1994, *L'avenir démolinguistique du Québec et de ses régions*, Québec, Conseil de la langue française: Les Publications du Québec (avec la collaboration de Jacques Ledent).

Thibault, P., 1980, *Le francais parlé: études sociolinguistiques*, Edmonton: Linguistic Research Inc.

Thomas, A., 1989, 'Le franco-ontarien: portrait linguistique', in Mougeon, R. and É. Beniak, (eds), *Le français parlé hors Québec*, Québec: Les Presses de l'Université Laval.

Thomason, S., 2001, *Language Contact: An Introduction*, Washington: Georgetown University Press.

Valdman, A., 1979, *Le français hors de France*, Paris: Éditions Honoré Champion.

Valdman, A., 1998, 'La Notion de Norme Pédagogique', in Bilger, M., K. Van des Eynde and F. Gadet, (eds), *Analyse linguistique et approches de l'oral*, Leuven, Paris: Peeters, pp. 177–87.

Vaugeois, D., 2000, 'Une langue sans statut', in Plourde, Michel, (sous la dir. de), *Le français au Québec: 400 ans d'histoire et de vie*, Québec, Conseil de la langue française: Les Publications du Québec, Fides, pp. 59–71.

Verreault, C., L. Mercier, et al., (eds), 2006, *1902–2002 La Société du parler français au Canada cent ans après sa fondation: mise en valeur d'un patrimoine culturel*, Québec: Les Presses de l'Université Laval.

Walter, H., 1998, *Le français d'ici, de là, de là-bas*, Paris: JC Lattès.

Weinreich, U., 1968. *Languages in Contact*. The Hague, Mouton, New York: Linguistic Circle of New York, (reprint of the original 1953 edition).

Weinreich, U., W. Labov, et al., 1968, 'Empirical foundations for a theory of language change', in Lehmann, W. P. and Y. Malkiel, (eds), *Directions for Historical Linguistics*, Austin: University of Texas Press, pp. 95–188.

Wesche, M., 1993, 'French immersion graduates at university and beyond: What difference has it made?', *Georgetown University Round Table on Languages and Linguistics 1992 Language, Communication and Social Meaning*, Georgetown: Georgetown University Press, Washington D.C., pp. 208–39.

Wesche, M., F. Morrison, et al., 1990, 'French immersion: Post-Secondary consequences for individuals and universities', in *Canadian Modern Language Review*, 4: 3, pp. 430–51.

Wilkinson, S., 1998, 'On the Nature of Immersion During Study Abroad: Some Participant Perspectives', in *Frontiers: The Interdisciplinary Journal of Study Abroad*, pp. 121–38.

Internet Sites

Bibliothèque et Archives nationales du Québec: www.banq.qc.ca

Centre d'Études acadiennes: www.umoncton.ca/etudeacadiennes/centre/cea.html

Commission des États généraux sur la situation et l'avenir de la langue française au Québec: www.etatsgeneraux.gouv.qc.ca

Commission de toponymie: www.toponymie.gouv.qc.ca

Commissioner of Official Languages: www.ocol-clo.gc.ca

Congrès mondial acadien: www.cma2004.com

Conseil supérieur de la langue française: www.clf.gouv.qc.ca

International Council for Canadian Studies: www.iccs-ciec.ca

Musée de l'Amérique française, www.mcq.org

Newspapers:

    Le Devoir: www.ledevoir.com

    Le Droit: www.ledroit.com

    La Presse: www.lapresse.com

Office québécois de la langue française: www.oqlf.gouv.ca

Privy Council Office: www.pco-bcp.gc.ca

Relations avec les citoyens et Immigration: www.immigration-quebec.gouv.qc.ca

Secrétariat à la politique linguistique: www.spl.gouv.qc.ca

Société nationale de l'Acadie: www.snacadie.org

Statistics Canada: www.statcan.ca

Supreme Court of Canada: www.scc-csc.gc.ca

Index

Modern French Identities

Edited by Peter Collier

This series aims to publish monographs, editions or collections of papers based on recent research into modern French Literature. It welcomes contributions from academics, researchers and writers in British and Irish universities in particular.

Modern French Identities focuses on the French and Francophone writing of the twentieth century, whose formal experiments and revisions of genre have combined to create an entirely new set of literary forms, from the thematic autobiographies of Michel Leiris and Bernard Noël to the magic realism of French Caribbean writers.

The idea that identities are constructed rather than found, and that the self is an area to explore rather than a given pretext, runs through much of modern French literature, from Proust, Gide and Apollinaire to Kristeva, Barthes, Duras, Germain and Roubaud.

This series reflects a concern to explore the turn-of-the-century turmoil in ideas and values that is expressed in the works of theorists like Lacan, Irigaray and Bourdieu and to follow through the impact of current ideologies such as feminism and postmodernism on the literary and cultural interpretation and presentation of the self, whether in terms of psychoanalytic theory, gender, autobiography, cinema, fiction and poetry, or in newer forms like performance art.

The series publishes studies of individual authors and artists, comparative studies, and interdisciplinary projects, including those where art and cinema intersect with literature.

Volume 1   Victoria Best & Peter Collier (eds.): Powerful Bodies.
            Performance in French Cultural Studies.
            220 pages. 1999. ISBN 3-906762-56-4 / US-ISBN 0-8204-4239-9

Volume 2   Julia Waters: Intersexual Rivalry.
            A 'Reading in Pairs' of Marguerite Duras and Alain Robbe-Grillet.
            228 pages. 2000. ISBN 3-906763-74-9 / US-ISBN 0-8204-4626-2